UNCUFFED

BULLETPROOFING THE LAW ENFORCEMENT MARRIAGE

DR. SCOTT SILVERII
LEAH SILVERII

Five
Stones
University

All Scripture quotations, unless otherwise indicated, are taken from the New American Standard Bible, ©1960, 1962, 1963, 1968, 1971, 1972, 1973, 1975, 1977, 1995 by The Lockman Foundation. Used by permission.

Other versions used are:

KJV—King James Version. Authorized King James Version.

NIV—Scripture taken from the Holy Bible, New International Version®. Copyright © 1973, 1978, 1984 by International Bible Society. Used by permission of Zondervan Publishing House. All rights reserved.

First Edition

Cover Design: Damonza Book Cover Designs

Editorial Team: Imogen Howsen

Interior Formatting: Five Stones Press Design Team

Publisher: Five Stones Press, Dallas, Texas

For quantity sales, textbooks, and orders by trade bookstores or wholesalers contact Five Stones Press at publish@fivestonespress.net

Five Stones Press is owned and operated by Five Stones Church, a nonprofit 501c3 religious organization. Press name and logo are trademarked. Contact publisher for use.

Dr. Scott Silverii's website is scottsilverii.com

Printed in the United States of America

DEDICATION

*We dedicate this labor of love to the spouses of law enforcement.
You're heroes behind the badge, and a fierce community who works
hard to keep your LEO in the fight and your family together.
Everyone's lives are much better for it.
Thank you.*

PRAISE FOR UNCUFFED

Uncuffed might be the most important book ever written specifically to help marriages in the law enforcement community. Crafted with tremendous transparency, raw honesty, practical application and a level of grit that could only be possible through their own harrowing experiences, our friends Scott and Leah Silverii have created a masterpiece that will undoubtedly help marriages everywhere. If you are a First Responder or married to one, this book will be a game-changer for your marriage!

Dave and Ashley Willis, Authors of The Naked Marriage and Hosts of The Naked Marriage Podcast

That is why a man leaves his father and mother and is united to his wife, and they become one flesh.
Genesis 2:24 (NIV)

CONTENTS

INTRODUCTION

There's an old saying that goes, "Happy wife, happy life." So when my wife, Leah, handed me the invitation to a big-deal writers' event, the kind where you have to dress up in a suit and tie and eat hors d'oeuvres that will never fill you up, I thought of a million excuses as to why we couldn't go, and then I smiled tightly and said, "Sure."

Suspicious, I asked, "Who's going to be there?" And then she said the words I dreaded to hear.

"There won't be any cops. It'll be good for you to meet other people."

I wasn't convinced.

As you can imagine, and have probably experienced, it wasn't long until I found myself with my back against the wall, eyeing the crowd as several husbands tried to engage me in conversation. As such things go, they noticed my tattoos and the way I watched the others, and timidly asked what I did for a living. Their eyes lit with excitement and they crowded in a little closer, and then they started asking the questions you and I love to avoid.

I answered questions patiently, my eyes continuing to scan the crowd, until one guy asked what was the toughest part of the job. I made eye contact, and he naturally shrank back a bit. My daughter says sometimes my eyes look dead, but we all know what cop eyes look like. You see them in the mirror every day.

"The hardest part of the job is coming up with a daily reason to live," I told him.

There was an awkward silence, and then he chuckled before taking a sip of his drink. The other men shifted from foot to foot nervously. To be fair, it wasn't their fault. They'd never committed to the oath and the shield, so why would I hold it against them? But he didn't let it rest.

"No, really," he said. "What's your real answer? What's the hardest part of the job?"

It was heavy conversation for an event that should have been light and fun, and I really hoped the group of women crowded around my wife were talking about something ridiculous and trivial.

I didn't have to think about my answer. There are times when people are uncomfortable with the truth, and this was one of those times. I explained that I'd never be able to unlive what I'd seen and done in my career. Not just the violent deaths, but being a witness to the suffering and brutality one human was willing to enact upon another.

The end result after a couple of decades behind the badge, was that the daily trauma made it harder to get up and face more of the same—and the temptation to eat a bullet and be done with it turned from a harmless thought to a real-life option.

No one can kill awkward party conversation like a cop can, so they found their way back to their wives, and hopefully it gave them something to think on next time they were pulled over by a patrolman.

It's a heavy topic, and not one I would've admitted to even a few years ago, but I've reached the point in life where I'm healed and I don't care who knows it or knows my struggles. Do you remember how I mentioned that truth often makes people uncomfortable?

Here's the truth—there's a reason law enforcement officer (LEO) couples rarely interact with non-LEO couples. You rarely have anything in common, and they don't understand the challenges unique to our world. I'm not saying we're better, but our relationships are different. Sometimes, very different.

Not only is meshing with non-LEO peers a challenge, but so is finding the help needed when our marriage is in trouble and desperate for rescue. We're notorious for not seeking help. We look at it as a sign of weakness, and when we go on the hunt for advice, we want it to be only what we want to hear.

Here's an uncomfortable truth—help doesn't make you weak, it makes you healed to fight longer and stronger for what you love most.

When Leah and I married, we'd both been divorced and knew the difficulties of blending families. We thought all of our prep time had made us ready to tackle the task.

What Leah didn't know was how tough marrying into a law enforcement life was going to be. In fact, it nearly ended our marriage. We had no one within law enforcement to mentor us, or walk us through the difficulties. And those who did offer their two cents suggested we chalk it up to a loss and move on to the next best thing. Looking back, it's only by the grace of God we made it through those dark days.

We wrote *Uncuffed* specifically for you and your wife. The marriage covenant you swore before God is more important than any oath you've ever taken, but you've got to put on marital Kevlar to bulletproof your marriage. Don't go into the fight of your life without protection.

You made it through the academy, FTO, and in-service trainings—you can make it through this. Leah and I want to share what we've developed through personal experiences, helping other LEO couples, and mentors who cared enough to tell us the truth.

Your marriage is special, but it's under attack. You can grow an incredible relationship if you're willing to set your sights downrange on what matters most, and make your marriage bulletproof. We've been there, we're still there, and we've got your six.

Blue Marriages Matter,
Chief Scott and Leah Silverii

1

PAIN AND HEALING

I'd already seen the crime scene, and seeing it again was the last thing I wanted to do. But I stood there and waited for my mayor to approach. He ducked beneath the yellow tape, and I watched the expression on his face change from confusion to horror. Sometimes it's hard for the brain to process what the eyes are seeing. The memory would be his burden to bear forever.

The crime scene was the worse offense I'd ever experienced. I was called out of church on a brutally hot Sunday in August to respond to what officers thought was a severed head lying on the side of the road.

One of my experienced commanders arrived to confirm that it was, in fact, a human head. A quick look into a pile of white kitchen garbage bags revealed the remains of a child's body. We'd later find out he was a seven-year-old bound to a wheelchair because of cerebral palsy.

The killer, who was the boy's father, leaned calmly on the porch railing as officers came to grips with what was going down. It was an open and shut case, but what remained was the reality of that Sunday afternoon. The murderer had dismembered his son while the mother was away. He wanted to make her feel stupid when she returned to see her son's severed head tossed on the shoulder of their road.

That reality is still hard to process. It's not something anyone should see, yet we've volunteered to stand in the gap for society and spare it from having to see for themselves. How do you go home to your wife and family after a Sunday afternoon like that? Sure, my body returned home, but my mind and my emotions had abandoned me. But guess what? I was back at work on Monday. We always go back for our next shift, no matter what happened the day before.

How do we return to the grind? How do we go home to our wife? How do we play with the kids? How do we move through life when there's so much death and cruelty concealed just below the surface?

Pain is an odd place to start off a book about marriage. But the truth is, we all have pain. Some process it, some medicate it, while some kill themselves to escape it. No matter how long you've been on the job, you are dealing with some wicked stuff that just won't leave you be. Maybe it wasn't a bad call; it might've been the office hazing, the cruddy supervisor, or the promotion given to someone less deserving.

But with all the cops I've mentored, the greatest source of pain comes from childhood. Whether they were abandoned, abused, or neglected, most of them can trace the clues to what they are struggling with in their marriage to a period in their past that left such an indelible mark that it still radiates destruction today.

When we begin identifying what attracted us to our wives, we usually list the easy stuff—looks, brains, work ethic, sassy, sexy. Once we grow closer, we begin to see the woman we love also complements our shortcomings. If we're willing to press in, we'll also understand that they become the one most able to help us heal from what ails us. God created us that way. But sometimes men, myself included, are a little hardheaded.

Where marriage suffers is when we fail to root out our source of pain, and then it manifests itself as dissatisfaction with our wife. No matter how helpful or understanding our wife is, until we see the darkness and bring it to light, there is no healing.

When Leah and I first began to mentor LEO couples, we would start with sharing biblical foundations of making marriage great. We soon realized that because of the prevalence of past trauma and current pain in either one or both of the spouses, the marriage information was falling on deaf ears. We quickly adjusted our focus toward helping them heal before we could help them grow.

Not starting with healing is like encouraging someone to do push-ups while both arms are in plaster casts. Pain comes in many forms, so let's take the time before we discuss anything else (like kids, sex, or finances) to make sure we are healthy and healed enough to develop a solid foundation for marriage.

Personal Profiles in Past Pain

You, my brothers and sisters, were called to be free. But do not use your freedom to indulge the flesh; rather, serve one another humbly in love. For the entire law is fulfilled in keeping this one command: "Love your neighbor as yourself."
Galatians 5:13–14

There are unlimited sources that cause pain. Most of the time it comes from childhood, prior relationships, recent trauma, and consequences of poor choices. The majority of the time we can trace its origins back to childhood incidents such as family dysfunction, abuse, neglect, or abandonment. Your pain, no matter how long ago it occurred, does matter.

What's really eating away at you? Are regrets consuming your thoughts? Can you sit in silence without a mental movie flooding your mind and demanding that you fill the quiet space with unhealthy thoughts? Do you stay busy just so your memories can't catch up with you?

Does the memory of your last shift ricochet in your mind, or is it the faces of those victims you simply cannot help? How about this: does the last argument or rejection by a supervisor continue to play out in mental scenarios until it becomes twisted into a fantasy of revenge?

You're not alone. The pain we carry from our past is tucked away and always available to muck up our lives or turn gold star moments into brown star disappointments. We allow pain, shame, and regret to overwhelm us with stress over how to cope with it. Unfortunately, the coping solves nothing. Healing does.

Have you developed your own secret way of helping to ease that hurt? Does your way involve something that, if exposed, would embarrass you, ruin your marriage, reputation, or cost you a career? If so, then you are not working toward healing, you are enabling the hurt.

Concealing weakness and unhealthy ways of managing it is a common practice for first responders. We avoid dealing with all types of pain, from physical ailments to emotional trauma. Is it good for us? Not always. But it's what we do. Our natural inclination that "I can handle it" squeezes out God's ability to restore us.

Why do we avoid God? Because the devil whispers in our ear that we're not worthy, and we can't trust God because all He wants to do is convict and punish us. If you haven't figured this out yet, the devil is the father of lies (John 8:44) and binding you to your past pain is his gain. Without a faith-led reliance in God, recovering from a past of hurt is going to be tough.

First responders are trapped with a double whammy, and our wives are victims to it. By the nature of our job, we are exposed to things that mess with our minds. Also, by the nature of the culture of our jobs, we are prohibited from seeking help in managing the trauma caused while doing the job. It's like going into battle without a medic.

Self-addressing deep pain has consequences and takes a toll on our lives. The bible gives us examples of the three ways we deal with pain:

Medication

King David was exalted as a great and mighty ruler. God Himself chose David to be king over Israel because of what He saw on the inside. David was a humble servant, and although anointed by God, he didn't come to the throne without serious personal baggage. David is a lot like us in carrying personal pain from our past.

Man looks at how someone appears on the outside.
But I look at what is in the heart.
1 Samuel 16:7b

David did his best to carry out his duty, but as with us, it eventually became too much to bear and soon cost him dearly. There are many ways to medicate our pain. Some of us use alcohol, drugs, sex, exercise, work, or any of many addictions to compensate for the hurt we feel from an emptiness caused by unresolved injury. King David relied on the most common form of "medication" for easing his past.

Because David preferred to seek a temporary fix instead of a permanent solution, his drug of choice was the flesh. Yes, even back before there was a thin blue line, sexual addiction was a major issue. As a matter of fact, David's sexual addiction caused problems for everyone associated with him. David's family suffered greatly because of his sexual sin, and a generational curse was cast upon his children.

David's pain was rooted in the rejection by his father, Jesse. He wasn't considered worthy of meeting the prophet Samuel who was sent by God to anoint a ruler. Yet, there in that rejected, messed-up boy, Israel had a king. David's rejection by his father stung and stuck. Have you been hurt by a parent, and never forgiven them? This injury doesn't heal in time.

Personally, I identify with David's rejection by his dad. My own father was a cold, physically intimidating man. He ruled his family with silence. His rejection, just like that of David's father, stuck with me. On one occasion as a kid way back in the seventies, I'd gotten a red warm-up suit with white stripes. It looked just like the one worn by my hero, Steve Austin, The Six Million Dollar Man (not the wrestler). I wore it everywhere.

One day my dad called out to me, but I was mixing it up with the neighborhood kids in the street, and didn't hear him. Then his words pierced the playful sounds of my friends: "Hey, idiot in the red suit, I'm talking to you."

I was about ten years old. I stuffed that tracksuit in the trash, and over forty years later, those words still hurt. When we have no affirmation as kids, we tend to grow up seeking someone to show us that we are loved and cared for. In David's case, he found that assurance in the women he slept with. Sex with one of his six wives wasn't enough. In addiction, it never is.

His pursuit of a married woman led to a child out of wedlock, the murder of the woman's husband, and a child who also would suffer greatly because of his father's rejection. Medicating your pain with anything other than actual healing is only going to make the problem more complex, and eventually it will cost you your marriage.

Motivation

Solomon was the son of David, and he was by far the wealthiest and wisest human ever to grace the earth. Despite being conceived from the affair his father had with Bathsheba, Solomon was loved by God and blessed tremendously.

The generational curse David incurred upon his family because of his failure to address past pain also caused personal suffering for his son. Solomon's wounds, as a result of family sin and the shame caused by the sexual affair of his father and mother, drove him to compensate in a very different way than David's medication.

Solomon's rejection by his dad and the shame he felt as a result of his family's "secrets" drove him to prove himself daily. Performance-based relationships are tough on us as kids and still difficult as adults. If you felt that you were only acknowledged and shown love when you made good grades, or behaved, or if you felt that you had to earn your parents' love, then you can relate to Solomon.

Motivation and achievements were Solomon's failed attempt to soothe his pain. The more he accumulated to fill the void of love and security, the less he felt deserving. In Ecclesiastes 2, he shares the futility of trying to outwork his hurt.

I've included this small section of the scripture, but I encourage you to read the entire chapter 2:1–24.

I denied myself nothing my eyes desired;
I refused my heart no pleasure.
My heart took delight in all my labor,
and this was the reward for all my toil.
Yet when I surveyed all that my hands had done
and what I had toiled to achieve,
everything was meaningless, a chasing after the wind;
nothing was gained under the sun.
Ecclesiastes 2:10–11

This is so personal to me, as I suspect it is to many of you. One of my first partners on the job was a good guy. We'll call him Jim. But to be honest, he could be a bit overbearing. As a rookie deputy, I struggled to purchase my duty weapon and all of the tools of the trade, as I'm sure we all did. But this guy had the best, most current, and most outrageously expensive gear imaginable. As a matter of fact, he owned two and three of everything.

Was he wealthy? No. He was probably worse off than me, but he needed to feel like the word he used to describe his latest weapon, motorcycle, or girlfriend: "Elite."

He conquered everything he touched, except the ability to humble himself so he could heal from his past. Just below the tanned surface of his rippling muscles were the tatters of a severely wounded soul. He'd been the victim of sexual abuse as a child, and his broken spirit drove him to over-portray manliness.

Along the way, he also suffered from divorce, bankruptcy, fathering a child in the course of an affair, and was eventually squeezed out of law enforcement. Still, he chose to rely on himself for getting out of a jam. Avoiding true healing and spiritual freedom through God's grace and mercy dooms us to an unending effort of emptiness and unsatisfactory results.

Our spirit requires peace, not prizes.

Meditation

There is a third unhealthy way of dealing with our hurt. Absalom was David's son and Solomon's half brother. His pain, like many with a dominant parent, began at home. Absalom also suffered from intense guilt over doing nothing to defend his sister from a sexual attack by another half brother.

How often do we find ourselves in a situation we know is wrong, yet we stand by silently as injustice unfolds? Acts of abuse or unfair treatment occur among families and friends. Being a victim or witness causes pain that, if not resolved, will continue to fester. This is especially true for acts of policy and legal violations we witness on duty, yet feel powerless to report.

Meditation stewed in Absalom's spirit until it boiled over into hatred. For two years he avoided confronting his feelings and the offender before it erupted in a rage, and he killed his half brother.

Absalom's deep-seated pain directed against his father, King David, also caused him to try overthrowing his authority. Absalom's desire to destroy his father led to his own death. Attacks against others is what defines Absalom. Are you feeling the rage of regret and wrongdoings roil beneath the surface while you look for an outlet to unleash your fury upon?

Sound familiar?

Which one of these examples are you?

Do you booze it until you lose it, yet it's worse than it began? Please understand that the substances used to fight addiction are not the problem. The problem is you're using addictive substances to avoid healing from your pain.

Listen up, Blue! Drinking, screwing around, and fighting will not heal your hurt. Don't listen to the devil. God's not waiting to smack you like a carnival game of whack-a-mole. You are good and you are worthy to be loved. God wants to heal you because He loves you. Allow yourself to heal. It's better than the hurt.

I love that old saying, "You can run from the police, but you'll just go to jail tired." You know there's a problem. Otherwise, you wouldn't be reading this book. It's time to stop avoiding healing and get serious about the long-term solution. Whether it requires confessing a wrong to your spouse, a friend, co-worker, or forgiving yourself for messing up once again, don't put off gaining the freedom from your past that you deserve. Your marriage depends on it.

2

PAIN PREVENTION

Pain is a part of life. It's unfortunate, and also unavoidable. My gut says you've had to deal with it, so now let's see how it affects our relationships. Marriage is two imperfect people coming together in an attempt to create a loving relationship, while working to help each other heal from their past. Because personal pain isn't as obvious as the physical, it can lie dormant, but destructive, for years and prove toxic to your relationship.

When Leah and I first married and I was no longer able to hide what was really bothering me, it caused my stress to spike. I was used to languishing in silence for a day or two whenever something traumatic happened at work. It was one of the ways I dealt with the pain. But with a new wife and family in the home, there were no longer places to hide in my own despair.

She couldn't understand why I wanted to be alone, and I was agitated that she wouldn't just go away. Yep, those were some pretty tough times in the beginning.

Whether you carry the stripes of being abandoned by a parent through divorce, the domination of one parent over the entire family, or you've suffered physical, verbal, or sexual abuse, law enforcement forces a suppression for healing while heaping new pain atop the open wounds of our past. This toxic combination weighs heavy on our marriages.

Let's identify these areas and walk through how to recover from them so your marriage doesn't become a victim to past or current offenses. Unlike physical harm, emotional, mental, and spiritual injuries don't naturally heal over time. While the body launches into an immediate recovery phase after experiencing a physical wound, your spirit remains vulnerable. As a matter of fact, those injuries get more severe the longer left unattended.

Time does not heal all wounds.

Left unhealed, it's easy for us cops to carry the pain into our high-stress jobs, day after day, with each wound making the ones before it even more intolerable. To combat this, we either block out all empathy for ourselves and our victims, or we flood each case assignment with an internal desire to make every wrong right in the victims' lives. Of course the reality is, we cannot control or prevent anything that occurs in the lives of others, yet we may carry the guilt of failing to protect them. This is especially dangerous because we tend to take out that guilt or frustration on "soft targets," such as our wife and kids.

Without the tools to process our own and secondary trauma, we enter the danger zone for cumulative PTSD. Where PTSD is concerned, there's a gap in understanding within the first responder community. The most well-defined awareness is for military service members after experiencing combat-related post-traumatic stress. This is usually the result of one or a few incidents of truly horrific experiences.

LEOs, as research has shown, are susceptible not only to the isolated incidents, but also to cumulative PTSD. This form is often more dangerous because it usually goes undiagnosed. Unlike a tragic incident, such as an officer-involved shooting that can be pinpointed, the daily grind that leads to the cumulative effect isn't realized until we're deep in over our head.

The damages of PTSD are exponentially increased when compounded by unhealed soul scars from past pain. Those who have experienced past pain often find that it increases the cumulative effects of PTSD, whereas someone without a painful history would not experience this.

Unlike limited exposure to trauma, cumulative PTSD may result from responding to high-threat calls for service like barricaded suspects, hostage standoffs, felony drug busts, natural, accidental, and homicidal deaths, and radio calls where someone has been seriously injured or abused.

I'll never unlive my first or final death on duty. It's not something we're conditioned to deal with, yet in between speeding cars and loudmouth drunks, come the dead and dying.

My first on-duty death experience was a call where I administered CPR to a retired cop. I worked like a madman alternating between breaths and compressions. He died. I was devastated and felt responsible.

My last on-duty death was a two-year-old girl who ran from her mother's grip in a shopping center parking lot. A full-sized pickup truck hit her and its front driver's tire crushed the little girl's skull. There was nothing the driver could've done. And there was absolutely nothing I could do. After almost twenty-six years on the job, I felt just as helpless as that rookie cop decades earlier.

But as you well know, it's not always the horrible calls for service that dump the most stress on us. Often, it's the difficult hours and shift work, overtime, being called in on days off for court, training, or case follow-ups. The anticipation of what and when the next call might be is an underlying source of anxiety that's compounded by the realities of those calls.

Dealing with other people's negative attitudes, or knowing that one slip of the tongue in setting them straight or taking up for yourself could see you before an internal affairs investigation adds enormous pressure. I've often said it was more dangerous in the office than out on the streets because of the politics and backstabbing among the brethren.

If you're determined to avoid the darkness of PTSD, you and your wife must be aware of what it looks like. Early identification is vital for getting the proper diagnosis and treatment in overcoming

PTSD. Too many of us say we'll get help later, but later may be too late.

Over the years, I knew something wasn't right. I wasn't myself, but that eventually became my new normal. Loved ones begged me to talk to someone. I knew the early signs, but worried that seeking help would be the kiss of death for my career. Besides, I worked twelve years of undercover and sixteen years in SWAT, and we did not show weakness. I used to joke that once I retired, I'd find help.

Eventually, I did retire, but it wasn't the life of leisure we imagine. Losing my identity as a cop was mixed with having to face the truths of what my life had always been about—pain. That first year in retirement was tough. I mean really tough. I ballooned up about fifty pounds to two hundred and seventy. Blood pressure, cholesterol, and all of the other diagnostics that signal a life in serious decline were taking shape in my golden years.

I bought new, bigger pants to hide the fat, but what I could no longer hide was the serious depression and suicidal ideation that accompanied the evaporation of our marriage. I wasn't the alpha man that Leah had once married, and there was nothing I could do to stop what PTSD was doing to me. I wanted to be and do better, but I wasn't able to. This time, my wife took the lead. She fought for me, forgave me, and refused to quit on me.

She drug me into a Christian counselor's office and never once apologized for it. I went in there ready to play the game. Say what he wanted to hear so I'd get a pass on the whole healing thing. It didn't take long until PTSD and past pain became the focus of our counseling sessions. It took a solid year of counseling to free myself of the demons of post-traumatic stress.

Being a hero is great. But being a stubborn hardhead is just selfish and dangerous. Seek help sooner rather than later. Here are physical signs of PTSD:

- Fatigue
- Vomiting or nausea
- Chest pain

- Twitches
- Thirst
- Insomnia or nightmares
- Breathing difficulty
- Grinding of teeth
- Profuse sweating
- Pounding heart
- Diarrhea or intestinal upsets
- Headaches

In addition to the physical signs that may alert you to the symptoms of PTSD, here are a few behavioral triggers that should alert you:

- Withdrawal from family and friends
- Pacing and restlessness
- Emotional outbursts
- Antisocial acts
- Suspicion and paranoia
- Increased alcohol consumption and other substance abuse

And finally, there will be emotional signs to help clue you into the reality that there is a problem:

Anxiety or panic

- Guilt
- Fear
- Denial
- Irritability
- Depression
- Intense anger
- Agitation
- Apprehension

PTSD has become almost chic among the alpha crowd. It gets blamed and credited for either too much or not enough damage in an officer's life. It's rooted in pain that can ruin a career and drive us to take our life. The truth to remember is the scars on our spirit will not heal until we allow them to be healed.

The first time my pastor said that to me, I was stunned. I thought who in the world would not want to allow themselves to be healed? It turned out I was one of those people.

There are several reasons first responders don't seek help. Intimidation and being ridiculed by others are the top two. You'd also be surprised to know that in this world of everything online, many of us don't even know where to get the help to heal.

Where do we begin? Most agencies offer anonymous call lines through insurance agencies. There are also numerous private groups, usually initiated by cops to help other cops get through the darkness. I always suggest that cops first communicate openly and often with their wives. Wives usually know already, but are too afraid to ask us about it. That's because they've been conditioned by how we shut them out, dismiss them, or deflect the conversation. And if they push too hard, we become angry. So they learn to walk on eggshells.

Don't be the strong, silent, and suicidal type.

Next, seek out the counsel of your pastor or agency chaplain. Many faith leaders are trained and focus their ministry on healing. If it's a situation requiring another level of care, they will refer you. Don't feel as though you're being passed around. Each situation is different and may require care ranging from conversation to medication. But you'll never know unless you're willing to trust someone to help you.

Disassociation Tactics

If you're suffering and don't think you can trust opening up to someone, then you're experiencing yet another reason why we first responders remain trapped in pain. It's called denial, and it erodes your marital Kevlar.

I know how important silence and isolationism is to our culture.

We rarely trust anyone who doesn't serve along the blue line, but this type of healing comes from God's spiritual realm where the only way to get help is to open up so you can be helped. Keep shoptalk inside the circle, but find someone on the outside to share your pain.

Cops will go to just about any length to avoid something we have zero interest or understanding in. One of the most common ways we do this is by suppressing emotions about the event. We can't hurt because we're warriors. Right? The best way to avoid the pain is to avoid the feelings associated with it. That's like saying if I ignore the blood running out of my chest, then the bullet that's in there will go away.

Disassociation is a tactic we use to distance ourselves from the act that hurt us. But even if the distance is physical space, the tether that ties you to it is always attached. Besides, you can't selectively shut off one emotion without adversely affecting other emotions. It's usually your wife who suffers when you try to manipulate emotional integrity.

Besides destructive behavior such as defensiveness, external influencers like drugs and alcohol exponentially increase the risk and damage caused by the pain. Bigger problems arise once our focus is now placed on fighting addictions, as opposed to healing the wounds that caused the hurt.

Here are three important emotions you must be aware of that are necessary and part of dealing with pain:

Anger

When you delay healing from pain through denial, you'll discover that anger has been waiting to rage for a while. This anger also has two options—to manifest internally or externally. Anger is usually directed at whomever it was that hurt you. If it was your dad, then you may seek out revenge, but please understand the consequences. Restoration is a much better option. In the absence of the original source of anger, we then zero in on whoever is closest and most vulnerable to our outrage—our wives.

Oftentimes, we turn that anger inward because we don't want to confront the offender, or show that we are vulnerable through being hurt. We begin to internalize shame, guilt, or depression for allowing ourselves to have been victimized.

Before you destroy yourself or your marriage, consider asking for help to process your anger. Smashing chairs in the house doesn't resolve your pain, it only leaves you with nowhere to sit. Seek help. Remember in either outlet, you are not responsible for what was done to you then, but you are responsible for how you handle it now.

Also, since we're giving good one-liner advice, anger is not a sin, as long as you don't sin in your anger.

"Be angry, and do not sin":
do not let the sun go down on your wrath,
Ephesians 4:26

Since we're talking about anger, I want to touch on a pressure point that harms our fraternity. Domestic violence is completely wrapped up in anger, pain, and shame. It's a desperate, dangerous cry for control.

Domestic violence committed by law enforcement, in particular, is experienced in at least 40 percent of police families as opposed to 10 percent of families in the general public. Experienced officers expose their families to domestic violence four times more often than other families. The truth you know as well as I do is that these studies are underreported because of our practice of handling things in-house.

If you are endangering your family because of your behavior, please don't blame it on your wife, the job stress, or the dog. If it's yours—own it. You need help immediately because it's an escalating pattern often leading to serious injury or murder-suicide. Most often, you're not mad at your wife; you're angry at your past. Allow yourself to heal.

Grieving

Grieving is important for allowing a balance to anger. It usually begins as the process of anger is resolved or managed. We usually don't bother taking the time to understand that grieving is a natural and necessary part of maintaining a healthy life. We're "go get 'em alpha heroes" who don't have time to grieve. But it's going to find us somewhere along the line, like it or not. Why not take the opportunity to manage it before things go too far?

Grieving isn't only a by-product of someone else's death. It might hit you when you transfer to another section and suddenly the crew from midnights is moving along without you. Maybe you missed out on a promotion, yet felt strongly that it was earned and deserved. You might be grieving the loss of your marriage, child visitation, or your job. All of these events are accompanied by emotion, and emotions require processes.

You may feel as though these days are your darkest and you can't hold on any longer. Allow me to assure you that you can make it to the light at the end of the tunnel. What's also great is that God has given you an incredible partner to make that journey toward freedom. Your wife is the best partner you'll ever have. Learn to lean on her when times are tough.

I've lost seven friends to line-of-duty deaths during my years in law enforcement. All were personal friends, and while I still miss each one dearly, I was able to grieve their passing to move forward and through the pain. Except one.

My best friend was brutally murdered in an ambush while on duty. A massive manhunt ensued before his killer was captured. I was my agency's SWAT commander, and requested activation to assist in the search across jurisdictional lines. A spiteful supervisor denied the request. The anger I felt toward my supervisor prevented me from grieving like I needed. Carrying the grudge of unforgiveness was tough until I came to understand that all I was doing was hurting myself and everyone I loved by not allowing the grieving process to move forward.

The truth is, there are crummy people in our profession. They will do things to hurt us on purpose. This causes so much stress and expands the open borders of pain we already harbor. Forgiveness is vital to not only liberating ourselves from them, but also giving ourselves the space to grieve.

Getting back to a healthy and happy you has been waiting, but the denial, anger, disassociation, and every layer of separation you placed between yourself and the reality of what harmed you has created a barrier. Now is the time to tear that wall down between you and the healing grace of Jesus Christ so that grieving personal pain may begin.

Acceptance

Rarely are we harmed by strangers. When the hurt comes from someone we know, the pain is so much more intense due to the loss of innocence and the betrayal of the trust we had in that person. There was an expected honor code of adult protector that was violated when the protector became the violator.

That violation not only left soul scars because of what action was perpetrated, but the trust was broken. The physical body can heal itself or be healed. Soul scars are very different, and responses to violations of trust hurt deeper than broken bones or bruises.

Moving beyond grief and into healing, we do begin to experience an acceptance of the ugly realities of life. No, we're not happy with it, but we do land on a level ground of peace or contentment.

I guess in a way, I needed to reach a point of acceptance after I retired from policing. I had so many big plans. I was no longer shackled to a job where an unrelenting and overly demanding public beckoned for my attention. It was time to soar. That first year was a dark, disturbing bust.

Although it was my decision to retire, I still had lingering hurt from the only job I'd known my entire adult life. It took time to decompress and process what had actually caused me pain, versus what were painful memories. I have reached a point of contentment, and have no regrets for my service or my retirement.

3

BREAKING FREE FROM PAST PAIN

Can you remain married yet still harbor deep pockets of past personal pain? Yes, you can, but why would you remain in bondage if there are avenues for regaining freedom? So many LEOs suffer with PTSD, poor health, anxiety, addictions, and depression. Your wife also suffers from the effects of secondary exposure to your hurting. Buried beneath levels of pain isn't the fertile soil for a happy marriage.

There are a few areas we'd like to discuss as you prepare to tackle the strongholds standing just on the other side of your freedom from past pain. The first is an important concept to understand—surrender. I know that most of us alphas think of surrender as waving the white flag. This isn't a case of quitting, but it is an opportunity to take a step back out of a losing battle to regain focus. Think of it as a reset, not a retreat.

Surrender

While putting up a valiant effort and resisting the enemy is encouraged, surrendering our lives to Jesus Christ is an act of love and trust. Sacrificial love is the highest expression there is. God gave up His one and only beloved Son so that we may know everlasting life through salvation. We are asked to surrender our sinful, selfish desires to God so that He may guide us to a deep relationship with Him, our wife, and others.

Why doesn't God just make us listen and obey Him, you might ask? That's a great question. God loves us so dearly that He gave us free will. How could we freely love someone if we were forced to do so? Free will is what separates us from the animals. Unfortunately, free will is also what's caused us all of our troubles, beginning with Adam and Eve.

We have the freedom to surrender to the one who will set us free from our troubled lives, or we can continue to cling to relationship after broken relationship.

> *You will know the truth, and the truth will set you free!*
> *John 8:32*

Soul Ties

Soul ties are God's invisible miracle of creating long-lasting bonds of relationship that go deeper than surface-level friendships. Have you ever met someone for the first time, and it was like a light popped on in your soul? I'm not talking about a romantic connection, but yeah, that happens too.

I think about the reaction when Mary went to visit Elizabeth in the New Testament. They were respectively pregnant with Jesus and John (the Baptist). Elizabeth's baby jumped in her womb at the sound of Jesus's mother, Mary. There was a tie between these two souls who would meet again thirty years later and change the history of the world.

> *As soon as the sound of your greeting reached my ears,*
> *the baby in my womb leaped for joy.*
> *Luke 1:44*

Another thought that I always associate with a positive soul tie is the brotherhood of David and Jonathan. David had six biological brothers, and Jonathan was the son of King Saul, who set out to kill David as he would become king of Israel. Despite both of these factors, these men were closer than brothers.

As soon as he had finished speaking to Saul, the soul of Jonathan was knit to the soul of David, and Jonathan loved him as his own soul.
1 Samuel 18:1

While soul ties can be positive bonds to old friends and family, they are also spiritual attachments to events, actions, images, or anything that has trapped you in that moment in time that just won't allow you to be free to move forward with your life. Sort of like the weekend shift!

Before I entered my basic police training academy, I was working at a place where I met a guy everyone called Ox. This dude was a big guy who had fled Cuba as a child and loved every second of his life. He'd just finished his senior season of college football, and was looking to get into law enforcement.

The instant we shook hands, we were brothers. Octavio "Ox" Rafael Gonzales stood in my wedding, we went to the basic training academy together, and spent several years working undercover narcotics until he moved to another agency to command his own unit. We continued to coordinate between agencies and through SWAT. We would've given our lives for each other.

On June 16, 2006, Ox was ambushed and murdered. I suffered to the point where I left law enforcement for a short while. The depression and anxiety over his loss left me unable to process through the grief. To say I loved him is an understatement. There was a soul tie that kept me tethered to grief and survivor's guilt. It wasn't until I was able to pray through that connection, and release myself from the negative, wrong aspect of his death, that I was able to put it into a proper context. It doesn't mean I miss him any less, but God never meant for the bonds of relationships to also carry negative consequences.

Soul ties can also start off bad and get worse. Maybe you were sexually assaulted as a child by a friend or relative. That sin-based connection has the ability to control the rest of your life because of the tether to a wrong relationship. Some other soul ties are bonded through addiction, guilt, and obligation, to name a few.

Anything that has attached itself to you and still influences your thoughts, emotions, or actions is a soul tie.

Satan is skilled at perverting our memories of past relationships. Have you noticed that when you and your spouse fight, how your mind starts to go back to past relationships? Maybe that ex-wife wasn't so bad. Maybe it was me, or I wonder if she's still available? The reason these thoughts take hold is because you've never severed them from your spirit. The good news is that you have the authority to pray over every one of the ties that keep you chained to the past, and slice right through them.

It's important that if you haven't already identified what it is that haunts you, to really begin praying over this. Ask God to reveal to you what it is in your spirit that you need to be freed from. You have the supernatural authority to cut negative soul ties.

Some of us visualize these spiritual ties as strands, like spider webs stretching from that moment in the past to where we are today. When I began to understand the concept of soul ties, I immediately saw my past pain connected to my spirit by giant suspension-bridge cables.

It might sound funny if this is your first exposure to the reality of soul ties, but once you begin to pray over them, you will start to "see" yourself still supernaturally connected to your past. Like I said, mine were so powerfully destructive over the course of my life that they were like thick, impenetrable cables. But, as I prayed God's authority over them, they were sliced like a hot KA-BAR through butter.

Too often, we also just blow it off. Most of us don't like going to a doctor when we're sick or hurt because we figure it'll go away or we can deal with it. Deceptive past reminders act in the same way. Can you live with the darkness of your past attached to your soul? Sure you can. Until you can't.

The point is, we can muddle through life without ever scratching that itch, or we can rid ourselves of the darkness, and move forward with living the blessed life that God created for us.

Inner Vows

Inner vows are common among most people. We make them as kids, teens, and young adults. They range from what we'll be when we grow up, to who we'll marry, to what type of job we'll secure. They also turn into negative attachments when we vow to never love again, never to be poor, to never spank our kids like we were spanked, and so on.

While these can be meant as aspirations and life goals, the critical point is that they can become destructive because of the emotional framework being erected outside of God's will for our life.

Let's take a quick step back and define just what an inner vow is so we're on the same page. According to Pastor Jimmy Evans, from his book *Freedom From Your Past*, they are a self-oriented commitment made in response to a person, experience, or desire in life.

When we are hurt, especially earlier in life, it's not uncommon to respond emotionally in anger with an inner vow to curse something or avoid the source of that pain. If we were whipped by a parent, and it embarrassed us, then it would be an expected response as a child to vow to never whip or discipline our own kids. While that might sound like a noble gesture at the time, the reality is that a parent who refuses to discipline will produce unruly kids without structure. Not to mention your spouse, who may grow frustrated by your refusal to take charge of the kids.

The truth is, you probably don't remember making that inner vow as a young child while on the receiving end of a leather belt. But the reality is, once you make these self-directed statements, you have the potential for igniting a pattern of dysfunction and misery.

Other common inner vows are:

- I'll never let anyone hurt me again.
- I'll never be poor like my parents.

- I'll never trust anyone again.
- I'll never discipline my kids.
- I'll never let my wife talk to me that way.

Do these sound familiar? You should take the time to write out your own in a bit, but for now, think through the times you may have purposefully or inadvertently made inner vows out of embarrassment, anger, or frustration. The danger is with the self-oriented intention.

Because we are focusing on freeing ourselves from past personal pain, inner vows not only imprint a pattern of self-reliance, but from the moment of that vow, we're tethered to that past event. The irony is that whatever you promised to escape, flee from, or avoid earlier in life, will usually continue to haunt you because you're chained to it via the inner vow. Similar to soul ties, they can and must be broken in order to move forward and be free from the effects of pain.

Healing and Light

For he wounds, but he also binds up;
he injures, but his hands also heal.
Job 5:18 (NIV)

Pain hurts, and it can also hurt to heal from pain. So many of us think that if we can just be happy for a while, then the pain will go away. Short-term thinking will never solve chronic pain. Actually, if you married with the hopes of a good wife being the answer to what ails you, chances are, you've now exponentially compounded your problems.

The good news is that we're often attracted to those we feel can help us in the healing process. It's part of the attraction process that God has designed so that we complement each other in our strengths and weaknesses. The best news, though, is that God is always at the ready to hear your cries for help and healing.

If you try to suck it up and play through the pain, what you'll eventually experience is that it starts to seep out at the most inopportune times. You'll become hypersensitive in low-priority discussions with your wife that lead to blowout arguments. Spikes in anger and lingering resentment will cause seeds of doubt to be planted in your mind about whether or not you married the right person, and well, you get the picture.

Unresolved pain occurs when we hold on to the hurt by refusing to forgive our spouse. It's not always the big things that create this deep agony between loved ones. But over time, things like misunderstandings, misspending of finances, cutting comments, or silent treatments start to build up.

Forgiveness is the immediate cure. When you screw up, apologize and ask for forgiveness. When your wife catches the short straw, make sure to forgive as you have been forgiven.

Law enforcement presents a serious challenge in hardening your exterior to trauma from outside forces. It also begins a desensitization process where your emotions become shielded as a form of self-preservation. It won't take long until this hard shell becomes a constant way of life. While you may notice the changes in the way of being better able to handle the horrific things humans do to each other, your wife only sees someone they no longer recognize.

Pain mustn't be allowed to drive a wedge between the two of you. It can become a barrier, not only in communication, but in the desperately needed intimacy you both need to remain a strong, united team.

LEOs often see the pain we suffer as a noble badge of honor. Like it's some righteous price we pay to protect the sheep. We expect civilians not to understand, and we don't bother helping our beloved to comprehend why we feel the way we do.

To be honest with you, most of us couldn't explain why we feel and act the way we do now as compared to before we became blue. My doctoral research allowed me to interview hundreds of cops all across the country, and the high majority of them had no clue why they felt that way either. They just attributed it to the stress of the job and the demanding culture.

One of the most common stories I heard was how the husbands

would have a hard day on duty thanks to either a traumatic call for service or the interoffice politics. The second they walked into the house, their unsuspecting wife would greet them and like a volcanic eruption, they'd go ballistic on their wife. She wasn't what pushed them off the cliff, but they sure landed on her head.

These same officers admitted that instead of apologizing and allowing their wife and them to heal, that they'd begin the silent treatment because they just didn't feel as though they had the tolerance to put up with yet another stressful situation. Of course that sent their wife into a spiral of pain and worry. It's a vicious cycle that causes deep, lasting scars unless healing is gained.

In addition to the pain we carry from our past, the additional stressors of not just the traumatic events, but the daily diet of negativity, both in the office and on the streets, cause an increased attachment to pain as a way of feeling alive. As LEOs gain experience and become societally disenfranchised, an emotional numbness becomes their standard. The internalized pain becomes a morbid source of feeling alive.

We have a choice to either continue on the path of unresolved pain and expect for it to deconstruct anything positive in our lives with an almost certain guarantee of dysfunction, or we can drop the rogue, bad-boy alpha routine and get the help we need to live a fantastic life as a loving husband and terrific cop. Trust us, your spouse will thank you.

The Healing Process

Like most things in life, there is a process involved with healing. Just in case you are curious why God doesn't snap His fingers and make your pain go away, it's important to understand the different types of healing.

Instant Healing by Miracle
There are countless examples of immediate healings performed by God or God through Jesus and His apostles. They were quick and seemed effortless.

Despite the various ailments, the common factor, besides God, was that those healed believed in the power to be healed. They were miracles, and occurred not because of how good or bad the person was, but because that was the process by which God chose to heal them.

Healing by Process

Whether healing is instant or occurs over a long period of time, it is the process for restoration. God may speed it up, or slow it down, but never forget that God sets the pace and the degree of restoration. What is important is that God's Word promises the end result, not how long it takes.

How often have we passed through a trial, and once it's over, we've either forgotten what we'd been through, or come to understand changes in our lives as a result of having gone through something? Part of God's healing process is education.

Remember when Lazarus's family begged Jesus to run to him? What did Jesus do? He took four days before He arrived at the tomb of His friend. Lazarus had even begun to rot and his flesh stunk, but Jesus was in no hurry. Why wasn't He?

There was a process. There were people besides Lazarus who would benefit in faith through this process, and while the end result was imminent, the process vetted out doubts, fears, and hope from those attached to the process. Read John 11:1–46 for yourself and mark down how many people close to Christ behaved less than faithfully.

Just as in the example of Lazarus being raised from the dead, there are feelings present during the process of healing. No matter how hard we try to pretend we don't have feelings, the truth is we do. It doesn't mean we have to weep at the coffee shop or during shift change, but the process of healing from past personal pain involves our being able to understand why we feel the way we do.

Our wives sense this hurt and the need to heal. They do not see this as weakness. Let me repeat this part—they do not see our need to heal as us being weak. That need is our humanity, and our loved ones desperately need to see that character trait illustrated in their LEO.

They know we are hard and tough enough to handle the streets, but they want us to be thoughtful and caring enough to allow for healing in our lives. This not only makes us better, safer cops, but we become the husbands that God ordained us to be.

4

BULLETPROOFING YOUR MARRIAGE

Back in my rookie days, I confused bulletproofing my first marriage with being bulletproof. Yeah, I was all into policing and about as deep blue as you could get. The job meant everything to me, and my marriage was there to support me and get me back on duty. I'd come home, unload the junk from that shift on her, and then I'd head right back to work. I had no clue she was suffering. She had no outlet for processing the drama I'd just fired her way. I assumed if I was happy at work, she was happy at home. I was very wrong.

It's ironic that we work in a profession where watching each other's back is vital to survival, yet in marriage we constantly drop the ball when we take our eyes off of our spouse. My sixteen years in SWAT taught me the value of specialized weapons and tactics for resolving high-risk scenarios. Marriage also requires the use of specialized resources for not only de-escalating tense standoffs, but as a daily tool for growing positive skills in a bulletproof marriage.

It wasn't until Leah and I found marriage mentors who took the time to teach us about the importance of having each other's back that our relationship began to grow indestructible. We call it "Having Your Six," and it's made the difference between just being married and having an incredible partnership as husband and wife. We want to share these six principles with you because not only are they simple to honor, but they will add marital Kevlar to your relationship like nothing else can.

Let's start with the reality that there is no such thing as the perfect marriage. You get out of it what you're both willing to put into it. Statistically, fewer people marry each year, yet the divorce rate remains the same. We marry with the hope of spending our lives together. No one says, "I do," to experience a mediocre marriage or the devastation of divorce. This is the beginning of that hope!

Having Your Six is based upon biblical truths, real-life experience and the fundamentals of shooting. Seriously, how could an old SWAT cop not relate marriage to range time? How cool that God allows us to use one of our policing skills as an illustration for marriage success. Because most men, including me, are visual learners, these six steps help us to clearly understand what is involved in making sure marriages remain shielded from harm or divorce.

Stance

This is where it all begins. Stance is so vital that it's one of the first items addressed in the garden of Eden with the very first marriage between Adam and Eve. You took an oath to stand with your wife in holy matrimony, now will you continue to make a stand with her in life?

The relationship you share with your wife was created by design to have no equal, outside of God of course. Not even your kids, your mom, or the cops in your squad should compare to the priority you place on your wife. Your spouse was designed to be your safe harbor and your fiercest battle buddy. Let your wife be your priority and everything else in life will fall into balance.

As cops, we use the excuse, "They just don't understand what I go through." Ever heard that one? I've never been to the moon, but it doesn't mean I wouldn't love listening to an astronaut talk about space exploration. It's the same thing with LEO couples. There's no reason to withhold from each other. This doesn't mean a massive data dump when you walk through the door after duty, but it also doesn't mean you should prevent her from the opportunity to share the events (good and bad) in your life.

I can guarantee, you're telling somebody about what happened on duty. It might not be your wife, but you are talking to a civilian. It's natural, and how we process. The reality is, whoever that person is, even if it's your high school bud or your parents, they are not your spouse. Your spouse stands by you and should be included in your daily life.

This is why God addressed men in verse 24: *"...a man leaves his father and mother..."* He knows our nature, and a big part of that nature is holding on to tethers that separate us from what really is important—our wife. It's not just in marriage, we do it with everything. We can't wait to get out of patrol, and once we're transferred or promoted, what do we spend our time talking about? What's going on back in patrol.

Can you be completely naked before your spouse?

Yeah, I thought that might get your attention. What we're talking about is being naked in complete openness, transparency, and accountability. It's impossible to say that your stance supports marriage when one or both of you have secrets. This is where so many marriages fall apart. We try to pocket our secret sins for later just in case. Secrets are intimacy killers, and no intimacy often leads to no marriage.

Those secrets develop because there is a space between spouses created when our foundational stance is out of whack. It's also where jealousy erupts into suspicion. Jealousy is not a bad thing. But we're not talking about keys-scratched-into-your-car-door type of jealousy. The righteous jealousy as God displays is healthy in a marriage. It's a protective posture once your wife is the focus in your life.

Jealousy is protecting what is yours. And to be very clear, you each belong to the other, and deserve to be fought over, not fought against. You do not belong to your friends, squad, or that old flame back in high school. You are two to become one. If you're not at the "oneness" stage yet, then this is the perfect place to be. It took Leah and me a while to understand it, and once there, it has changed our lives and marriage.

We naturally begin to drift toward what interests us. Some lean toward career and achievement, while others focus on the home and family. There's nothing wrong with these pursuits unless they knock you off balance.

It's important to remain aware that your spouse is the most important person in your life. Everything else will fall into place when you show her that you are committed to remaining grounded in a stance based on God's Word for honoring her and the marriage.

How to improve your stance:

Remain on solid, level ground so that your decisions are based on truth and not temptation or emotion.

Keep both feet on the ground by understanding that your stance affects your wife. Remaining grounded allows her to know she is safe and secure in your relationship.

Allow both knees to remain bent and flexible so that you can respond and adjust to the changing seasons and challenges that life brings into marriage.

Grip

I recall one of the first problems I had on the shooting range as a rookie cadet was that I was strangling the life out of my weapon. I was so afraid that old .357 cannon was going to blow back over my head like I'd seen on TV and movies that I squeezed as tight as I could. The reality was that I was reacting out of fear. I'd never shot a .357 revolver, and up until that point, no one had ever taught me how to shoot based on knowledge and experience rather than my misguided experience of nothing more than misinformation.

Once I understood that shooting, just like marriage, requires an active hands-on approach rather than trying to dominate or control, everything improved. Most couples make the mistake of thinking that after the big wedding blowout, we simply do marriage. Then, when problems arise, and they will, we either try to control it like a radio dispatch call to arrest battling brothers at a drunken family reunion, or we go hands off. Neither works for marriage.

Once we've committed to the proper, solid stance of having our wife's six, we must apply the proper grip for addressing each situation as a team. The best way to know how to handle challenges is by talking to each other about the problem. We're too quick to jump in and try fixing it every time our wife expresses frustration. Sometimes, they don't want or need us to fix it. They simply want us to listen. Other times, we're the problem and require adjusting our own grip. No matter what the hurdles are in your relationship, a willingness to properly apply an active hold of the solution shows that you are engaged in working together toward peace and a solid marriage.

A final word about grip. We are told often that one of the reasons spouses drop a shot is that they claim to have fallen out of love. You can no more fall out of love than you can become a cat. Love is not a feeling to ebb and flow. Love is a choice. Saying you fell out of love and now want a divorce is like selling your gun because you ran out of ammo. No, you don't give it up, you take hold, dig in, and reload.

Sight Picture

We're going to focus on this as it relates to seeing marriage for what it really is. If yours is messed up, then set your sights on making it right. If you're blessed with a powerful relationship, then amen for both of you, but let's continue to focus on keeping it tight and protected.

A big part of having proper sight picture is having the single vision of relationship. You focus on one target, and that is your marriage. If you start looking elsewhere, this is when your aim is off and bad things happen. Part of that single vision focus on marriage is understanding that you and your wife now share everything in life.

The old joke about what's yours is mine and what's mine is mine unfortunately still holds true in many LEO marriages. When we enter into a marriage covenant with God, sole possession of everything, and we mean everything, goes out the window. Your money, your debt, your favorite chair, your guns, your addictions, your magazines, your kids (yes, we said kids), your sins, and even your own body no longer belong solely to you. Remember when we talked about the two becoming one (Genesis 2:24)? Well, this is where it happens.

The husband should fulfill his marital duty to his wife, and likewise the wife to her husband. The wife does not have authority over her own body but yields it to her husband. In the same way, the husband does not have authority over his own body but yields it to his wife.
1 Corinthians 7:3–4

God has established a marital chain of command with Him as the head, then Christ, the husband below, and the wife following her husband's spiritual headship. This scripture is where we often get the disgruntled scoffs from the wives because it may appear at first look that the husband is the boss.

Nothing could be further from spiritual reality. Servant leadership and sacrificial love distinguish the marital chain of command from the world's understanding of being the boss.

But I want you to understand that the head of every man is Christ, the head of a wife is her husband, and the head of Christ is God.
1 Corinthians 11:3

The key is to show that through submitting one to another, we surrender ourselves so we each hold equal possession of everything. Two-as-one also isn't saying we have $100 in the bank, so we each get $50 bucks. That's splitting community property. A true sight picture sees that you both have ownership of the same $100.

It's not uncommon to bring self-preservation tendencies to the table after you've been burned in a prior relationship. Escaping divorce with the soft body armor on your back forces us to develop a protective perspective of not losing what little survived while fleeing the fire of a failed marriage. It can make us hesitant to lay out all of our chips.

But repeating past mistakes isn't the way to see this relationship grow. Having a single sight picture is the key to freely giving of yourself to your wife. Whether it's time, talent, or cash; there's always a reciprocating benefit to giving of yourself. Now it's time to give up any selfish visions you my have that no longer contribute to protecting your wife's six, and look downrange together at a beautifully strong relationship.

Breath Control

Law enforcement is situated as society's moral entrepreneurs. We didn't ask for it, but through the years, it's been left to us to decipher not only what is criminal, but also what is moral, ethical, and acceptable. Think about how many calls for service we respond to that have nothing to do with criminal law.

One of the big conflicts of holding this position is that we aren't always the brightest examples of personal control. I mean, from a cultural portrait, cops live a rough life—we're prone to the guns and tattoo attraction, sexually liberal in actions, faith-based behavior takes a back seat to personal preference, and marriages can end before an academy class graduates. I'm not knocking the fraternity, but let's take an honest look at the big picture. Self-control isn't a dirty word, yet it has a negative association with being boring and dull.

Breath control helps us block out all of the external distractions while getting a grip on internal stressors that pull our stance off balance. When we practice personal control it allows our wife to feel secure which increases trust and affection. That often increases intimacy, i.e. sex. God designed sex to be pleasurable for the married couple. He isn't a prude when it comes to the marriage bed, but He expects that it not be defiled.

Let marriage be held in honor among all, and let the marriage bed be undefiled, for God will judge the sexually immoral and adulterous.
Hebrews 13:4

When we begin to lose control of what is right and honorable within the parameters of a strong marriage, temptations seep in that lead us to set our sight picture elsewhere. This obviously has the potential to lead to emotional and physical affairs. In this environment, there is no marital accountability because we've allowed our breath control to run rampant until we're hyperventilating on sin and temptation. We'd like to share a few ways to promote personal control through an atmosphere of accountability:

- Think before saying and doing.
- Own your mistakes.
- Consider decisions and consequences.
- Pray God's grace in resisting sin.
- Confess, repent and restore.
- Promise that divorce is never an option, and mean it.

Exercising breath control simply means taking the time to step back and gain an objective perspective toward your relationship. What areas can be improved, eliminated, and confessed for healing and new growth? Keeping an even keel based on thought-through decisions creates a protective Kevlar barrier around your relationship. Practicing personal restraint under the critical eye of the public and your co-workers also safeguards you and your wife from the effects of malicious attacks.

Trigger Control

One of the trainers during my FTO phase was a little less than KA-BAR sharp. A new sergeant determined to make a name for himself got just what he was looking for. Although the name wasn't what he was hoping for. We'd responded to a shots-fired call from inside of a residence. We talked about it being a possible suicide, burglary, or domestic gone very bad, and how we'd strategically respond.

The sergeant made such a show "tactically" heading to the door that I thought we'd never actually cover the twenty yards from his siren-blaring cruiser to the victim's home. It wasn't like surprise was his goal. Once we made contact with the homeowners and secured the location, we were told that the pistol had just gone off. It struck the husband in the fleshy part of his gut, but was going to require a trip to the ER and a few stitches.

Fresh from the academy and many days on a firing line with an old revolver, I knew enough to realize that the gun didn't just shoot itself. It required trigger control, or in this case, a lack of it. While continuing his routine for everyone's benefit, the sergeant decided to examine the weapon himself. As he looked down the barrel and spun it back and forth, he fired off another round that believe it or not, struck the husband in the other side of his portly potbelly.

Yep, trigger control was the word of the day, and while I can't tell you what we called the sergeant because he's still on duty as a guard in the prison, let's just say it was fitting.

But how does trigger control apply to your marriage? Well, the key here is that a projectile doesn't just pop out of a barrel on its own. Neither do arguments with our wife. There's a process that has begun before that bullet streaks across space to strike its target. Too often we find ourselves at each other's throats without even understanding why. How often have you two argued and an hour later all you can recall is that you're mad, but not sure why?

Those emotions that roiled up until exploding like hot lead from the chamber of a negligent discharge had to have been ignited through a process. This is where understanding marital trigger control is important for ensuring there are no casualties in marriage.

Thinking back to what it takes to actually fire a bullet, we can see that there must be a grip on the weapon. Has that grip been dominant over the marriage, or loosely handled while your focus was elsewhere? Next, the trigger can't pull itself. It requires tension. What type of tension is in your relationship? Has it been brewing for a long time, or was it something that flashed hot and angry over an unresolved issue?

Once tension causes the trigger to engage, the hammer drops to strike the primer. Have either of you made a practice of dropping the hammer on one another with suspicions, allegations, or unconfessed secret sin? If so, then don't be surprised when the primer ignites to rocket that projectile through the barrel and straight for each other's hearts.

There are so many ways to defuse shots fired in anger, but unlike that former sergeant, seldom does a gun just "go off." Here are a few ways to practice marital trigger control. There's an old SWAT maxim that applies here.

Contain—Make sure you don't increase the intensity or allow the situation to branch out of control. Focus on the facts as they are, and take the time to completely understand what the issue is about before launching into an attack or unjustified defense on an unrelated topic.

Control—Remove emotions from running the show. Understand that love is not an emotion. It is a choice. With this foundation, make sure that you choose to respond with facts. Facts can include the reality that you're experiencing tense emotions such as hurt, anger, despair, but don't allow them to drive your reaction.

De-escalate—Your wife is your partner, and not some street-level encounter. It's easy to ramp up the intensity for the sake of dominating an argument, but if you "win," you actually lose. Practicing trigger control to avoid high emotional conflict will result in a more productive disagreement and promises to resolve the conflict quicker with both of you feeling better about resolution.

A soft answer turneth away wrath: but grievous words stir up anger.
Proverbs 15:1

Follow-Through

How often do we say we're going to do better but fail to do it? It applies to diet, exercise, studying for the sergeant's exam, or treating your wife as if she really is the most precious person in your life. I'm not judging. I've said I would but I didn't so many times that I'm immune to calendar alerts and reminders left around my office. Then the guilt kicks in, and I feel even worse for doing whatever it was that I said I wouldn't do. Ever been there?

The apostle Paul was the best of the best. He was renowned for his discipline and faithfulness. To put it in modern times, the dude was a stud. But, although he loved Jesus and lived his life to serve Christ, Paul was also the very same thing that we are—human. Now, that's not an excuse to mess up in marriage or life, but it is a reality we must be aware of.

We want to have our wife's six, because she's our partner in this life. When we place her as our priority in life everything else falls into place. But only saying it and failing to follow through is as meaningless as a bullet fired into the dirt berm.

Look at what Paul says about wanting to do right, but still doing wrong. This is an incredibly powerful and humble admission. We should really use Paul as a guide in our walk.

I do not understand my own actions. For I do not do what I want, but I do the very thing I hate. Now if I do what I do not want, I agree that the law is good. But in fact it is no longer I that do it, but sin that dwells within me. For I know that nothing good dwells within me, that is, in my flesh. I can will what is right, but I cannot do it. For I do not do the good I want, but the evil I do not want is what I do. Now if I do what I do not want, it is no longer I that do it, but sin that dwells within me.
Romans 7:15–20 (NRSV)

So how do we follow through honoring the principles of Having Your Six? Start by being aware of your own limitations. Stop running behind a façade of macho bravado when in reality you may feel alone, afraid, or concerned about your marriage. Express yourself and allow your wife to help walk you toward reassurances with the relationship, the job, or your future vision.

Don't hesitate to show her how you feel. If you think she's looking especially great that day, tell her immediately. Text her that you love her at any time you feel it. Don't play the strong silent type and leave her guessing how you actually feel. Make it obvious. Very obvious.

Our pet peeve is when people tell someone, "I love you more than you'll ever know." I mean, what kind of bull is that? Why leave them hanging? Follow-through is as important in marriage as it is in preparing your body to squeeze off the next round from your trusted duty weapon.

The key here, as in all six of these bulletproofing principles, is that you and your wife are a team. There is no one else better suited for you than she is. You have so much authority for helping your wife become the woman of your dreams. Praying for her is the best way to start, but by practicing each of the Having Your Six principles allow her to see that you are completely committed to her and your marriage. You're a natural doer and fixer on the job. You fight for people you don't even know, so focus that fighting spirit on your relationship. If it's not where you want it to be, then work to make it right. If it's pretty good, then work to make it great. Trust these six bible-based principles, and you will bulletproof your marriage.

PINK LIGHTS / BLUE LIGHTS

If you'd asked me about meeting my biggest needs in marriage years ago, I would've said something about sex or money. Most men would reply with something similar: sex, money, friends, a big party at their wedding, or job security.

What if I told you none those things are even close? As a matter of fact, most of those things drive us in the opposite direction from what is the most important thing in marriage. Here's the truth, your personal relationship with God is the single most important thing in your marriage.

God didn't create marriage for bridal showers and bachelor parties, but to share in a relationship. Since He created marriage for relationship, wouldn't you think relationship would be the most important thing in your marriage? Sure it is. But the marriage covenant is only successful when it honors God's plan for you and includes His presence in that relationship.

The reason we've focused on your relationship with God is that without Him, you're going to place the burden of your satisfaction upon your wife. The same goes for her in her relationship with God. No matter how amazing you or your wife may be, neither of you will ever be God. What happens when you become unhappy in your relationship and begin to doubt that your wife was the right one for you?

If we fail to set God at the tip of the spear, we're going to become unsatisfied with our spouse, no matter how fantastic they actually are. Unmet expectations are the main cause of divorce. Can you imagine expecting God, and having your spouse try to fill that role? It's not fair to them and it sure isn't biblical.

And then the cycle starts. You get disappointed by that person for not being perfect, so you move on to the next one, and the next one, and the next one. The grass is never greener.

We all have an innate desire to know God, even if we don't have a close connection to Him. It's implanted in our spiritual DNA. Most of us spend time searching for satisfaction from others. We're all imperfect people and will always disappoint each other at some point. This is because we unfairly elevate people as our god (lower case *g*) in place of connecting first with God the Father. This is where unmet expectations occur, which in marriage, leads to divorce. Placing God first causes your marriage to last.

Her Needs

We're going to state the obvious, and then we're going to discuss what society thinks is obvious, but based on the divorce rates, incidences of police family domestic violence, and inter-partner chaos, we're going to talk about reality.

Men and women are different. You're probably thinking, "Duh," at this point, but sometimes, especially in this day of social equality and feminism, we tend to forget something so basic.

Just because men and women are different, doesn't mean they aren't equal. They are. The meshing of these two truths has given rise to conflict and confusion from the very beginning. I think the jumping-off point is caused by the second chapter of Genesis when man is formed before woman. Although that might mean seniority gets preference in police life, it's not the same in marital life.

Let's back up to the first chapter of Genesis to understand just how equal man and woman are by perfect design. God didn't fashion Adam to resemble Him, and then toss in Eve as an afterthought. The word *Adam* in Hebrew means man, or mankind. When God refers to creating man in His image, He is saying the creation of mankind. There are two genders in the creation that make up mankind—male and female.

Walking this through, God created mankind, which was man and woman. God's holy hierarchy (chain of command) sets man as the spiritual head of the household. Not as boss, but as servant leader. Woman was created from man (from one became two) to show that once they marry into a covenant relationship with each other as we have with God, the two become one. Both equal, but very different.

So God created man in His own image; in the image of God He created him; male and female He created them.
Genesis 1:27

Part of that difference involves the way each gender internalizes external forces, and the way they relate to one another. Too often, we spin our wheels trying to change one another, when instead our best efforts would be invested in trying to understand what makes each of us unique and special. The differences were by design to attract us to the opposite sex and complement each other's deficiencies.

Instead of asking what's wrong with them, we should be asking whether or not we're willing to meet their needs. Women have very different needs than men do. It doesn't mean either is right or wrong, but different by heavenly design. There are five basic needs that speak to a woman's heart.

Love
Women need love. So much so, that men are commanded to love their wives.

Husbands, love your wives, just as Christ also loved the church and
gave Himself up for her.
Ephesians 5:25

Your wife needs to hear you say, "I love you." Just because you said it once six years ago during the wedding doesn't mean she's covered for life. You've got to fill her love tank. Not once, but every day. That's how God made women.

Here are some great ways to fill your wife's love tank:

- I love you.
- You're beautiful.
- You're a great mom.
- You can do anything.
- I'm so proud of you.
- I'm so lucky to have you.

I'll be the first to say that women are tough. LEO wives are especially tough. But don't take that for granted. God created women to love and nurture, and you need to recognize that through how you treat her. It's easy to crush your wife's spirit with thoughtless or negative words. Your man mind is just thinking she's sensitive. Well, yeah! She is!

When you fight, your wife needs to be reassured that you love her and that you're not going anywhere. I promise, those thoughts go through their heads. When you speak words of love to your wife, this gives her Security, which is another need that speaks to a woman's heart.

Security

Women speak the language of security. They need to know that there is safe harbor in the storms of life, and that no matter what, you will be there with them and for them. We provide that refuge when we love sacrificially as Christ did.

Another way to shore up her place of refuge is by paying attention to her words so you will understand and anticipate her basic needs. Never make her ask to have her needs met—we must take the lead and it'll pay off in relational dividends beyond belief.

You're probably thinking, "Well, Scott, how in the world am I supposed to anticipate her basic needs? I'm not a mind reader." No, you're not, but God did give us some direction. Here are three examples:

Headship

Christ should always be the example of a loving head of the household. Too often we men assume it means we get to boss everyone around and dominate our wives. That is absolutely the wrong mindset. I always liked the illustration of the difference between "Go" versus "Let's go."

Man is ordained to be the spiritual head of the family. This is a gender-assigned responsibility from God. Leadership can and should be shared by both of you. Leah is a better money manager while I'm a self-described man of action. I'm comfortable and supportive with her taking the lead on finances. You should also encourage your wife's special skill sets. Let's face it, there are a lot of cop wives who are leaders out of necessity. Who else is going to keep a household running when you're gone on extra details and holidays?

She can be a leader in your home without threatening your headship. Embrace this. The two of you will be stronger for it. Let me give you a tip. The next time your wife seems overwhelmed, ask her what you can do to lighten the load. Offer to pay the bills or do the budget, offer to take the kids to whatever activity they've got. Being the head of the household means active participation—it doesn't mean you come home from shift and put yourself in front of the TV with a cold one until you have to go back on duty.

Sacrificial headship will guide you in meeting your wife's needs in a loving, responsible and mentoring manner. Praying together is one of the most effective ways of coming into this posture. We'll leave you with this verse that is a great guide for being there for her.

Husbands, love your wives, just as Christ loved the church and gave himself up for her to make her holy, cleansing her by the washing with water through the word, and to present her to himself as a radiant church, without stain or wrinkle or any other blemish, but holy and blameless. In this same way, husbands ought to love their wives as their own bodies. He who loves his wife loves himself.
Ephesians 5:25–28

Communication

If we opened up and talked in detail and with enthusiasm with our wives like we do in the squad room, the divorce rate would be a lot lower. To say that men only give terse, guarded responses is a myth. I've seen cops in the squad room gossip more than the biggest Chatty Cathy. Cops know everything about everyone in the department, and they talk about it with relish. The juicier the gossip, the better. It's part of the LEO culture. I'm not saying it's right and doesn't need to change. I'm just saying it is what it is.

But our conversations become guarded when certain topics are broached. It's easy to talk about other people, not so easy to talk about ourselves. Especially when it concerns areas of our lives that…wait for it…stir up feelings we haven't processed yet. Your wife wants to know every part of you—the good, the bad, and the ugly. She's your safe place.

If you must, put yourself in the same state of mind you use while interviewing a witness or victim. Dedicate uninterrupted time to talk. Eliminate all distractions (ahem…cell phone, cell phone, cell phone) and actively listen to what she says. If she asks questions, answer them. Also, whether you feel like it or not, respond with full details. This shows that you value her, which helps make her feel secure.

Nonsexual Touching

We guys usually associate physical touching with sex. It's how our brains are wired. She touched me! Time to strip down. Look, I get it. I'm a guy. There was a time when, if Leah would high-five me while passing in the hallway, I'd start peeling off clothes and running for bed.

Let's say it together this time—women are different from men. They just don't respond the same way we do. Women are slow cookers and men are microwaves. While touch is important, it shouldn't always be initiated by men as a trigger for sex.

A gentle touch, a hug, shoulder rub, or just holding her in your lap without her have to dodge your octopus hands creates security and intimacy for your wife. That nonsexual intimacy goes a long way toward fanning the flames into something more passionate. But the key to meeting your wife's needs is the love, care, and touch given in steady doses throughout the day.

His Needs

This section is for the women, but husbands are welcome to follow along. There's an old joke about the difference between the perfect date night for a husband and wife. The wife's perfect night starts with fancy clothes, flowers, and dinner by candlelight, followed by a moonlit stroll before being carried over the threshold and kissed softly. The man's perfect date night is a little different. All he requires is for his wife to show up naked holding a six-pack.

Are we that simple? Well, I'd like to think not, but it doesn't mean we need complication for maturation. It also doesn't mean our differences will divide us. We were created on purpose with a spiritual intentionality. In other words, God created those differences to complement each other so that we'd remain in a posture of surrender.

While it may require more than a naked wife and beer, each spouse is happiest when their needs are being met. Is your husband's dream date the same as yours? This is unselfish love. Focusing on each other's needs instead of our own will put your marriage on track for peace and fulfillment.

God commands men to love their wives. But there's a second part of that verse. He commands women to respect their husbands. These are commandments because it's not the natural inclination of men to love. God gave that characteristic to women. And it's not the natural inclination of women to respect. Thus, He commands us to do what doesn't come natural. Why'd He do that? So we'd come to Him for the abilities to do so.

I'll say it again. Women and men are different. One of you needs love and the other respect. Don't try to fill your husband's tank by telling him you love him all day. That's what fills your tank. Your husband is designed to run on respect.

What does respect look like?

- I'm proud of you.
- You're a good provider.
- Thank you for everything you do for this family.
- You're amazing at _____.
- How was your duty?
- Can I pray over you today?

Think of his time on duty. We deal with the public's problems more than we handle our own. We'll remain engaged with even the most abusive jerk to help get their problems solved, no matter how long it takes. But once they start to disrespect us, it's time to move along. It's not that we men have to be exalted as kings, but we naturally repel efforts and words that make us feel like we're not worthy.

Because that's the language we speak, men will move toward the place or person where we feel we are being respected. It may not seem like a big deal to you, but when we men are criticized for not doing or being unable to do something, we immediately default to failure mode. We know you're just trying to "help" and "nurture," which is what God designed you to do. We men know we can be better, so don't stop trying to nudge us there.

Sure, but this goes back to the garden of Eden. God made male and female. He didn't create two identical beings to do life together. He created two very different people because they complement each other. Just because you'd do things one way, or handle something one way, doesn't mean your husband will react how you would. Instead of criticizing for where he isn't, build him up to where you want him to be.

In full disclosure, I wasn't overly engaged with the kids when Leah and I married. Sure, I was happy to give orders and assign chores, but attending to their hearts was where I needed to focus. Leah didn't rip on me because she knew that wasn't where I was naturally gifted. Instead, she would encourage me and thank me for being there for the kids. It made me feel respected and appreciated, even though I wasn't comfortable doing it. Soon, it became one of the things I enjoyed taking the lead on, and it gave Leah a great sense of security in seeing how I attended to the little ones on a more intimate, caring level.

LEOs are usually alpha males who by nature are fixers and doers. We don't respond well when that energy is diminished. Instead, we're more apt to try harder when it's harnessed in a way that focuses our alpha gift toward the marriage and family.

Just like you wives, we men have basic needs beyond a bass boat and a mega remote control. It's important for men to understand that our needs can't be met by material things or other people. Pursuing the spiritual desire of our heart will give us a satisfaction that bigger, better toys cannot.

Honor

Look how perfect this circle is; we go back to Ephesians 5:22–24. This is the model that works because it is the model God created for us to not only love and honor each other, but to also love and honor Him.

Wives, submit yourselves to your own husbands as you do to the Lord. For the husband is the head of the wife as Christ is the head of the church, his body, of which he is the Savior. Now as the church submits to Christ, so also wives should submit to their husbands in everything.
Ephesians 5:22–24

One of the best ways to honor your husband is to allow him to make mistakes (unless self-destructive). Now, the second part of this is not to criticize him for the mistake. Men like forging a path, and although we rarely admit it, we self-reflect and accept the lessons learned at our own expense and at our own pace. It's a process.

Sex

Men and women usually have very different sexual needs and drives. Desire discrepancy isn't as serious as it sounds, but it is another fancy way to say you both usually get frisky at different times and respond to different stimulations. Waiting for the moment when you're both in the mood will limit your sex to somewhere between very seldom and never.

Men typically have a higher sex drive than women. That's not always the case, but for the majority of men, that's true. This goes back to unselfish love. We talked about how women are slow cookers and men are microwaves. Women are dealing with jobs, kids, activities, and who knows what else. It's easy to make those things a priority. Sometimes you don't want to have sex, but your husband still has needs. Just like he should meet your needs with communication, you should meet his sexual needs.

The wife does not have authority over her own body, but the husband does. And likewise the husband does not have authority over his own body, but the wife does. Do not deprive one another except with consent for a time, that you may give yourselves to fasting and prayer; and come together again so that Satan does not tempt you because of your lack of self-control.
1 Corinthians 7:4–5

It's important that you both discuss sex, and in particular, his needs and how you can meet them. When sex is used as a reward or a weapon, only bad things can ever result. Sex was created by God as the seal of His marriage covenant, so enjoy it. A lot.

Friendly Fun

On the job, cops seek out confrontation to bring peace and order. We get the radio call that a problem is at hand, and we're off to inject ourselves into it until a solution is found. Yet we avoid confrontation and resolution at home. We believe it's because we'd prefer to avoid it, but the reason we get involved at work isn't to prolong the confrontation between strangers, but to end it.

Because of this aversion to conflict, we are more productive when the time spent with our wife remains light and loose. That doesn't mean we don't address serious issues, but men don't do drama well. We open up more as the scenario remains nonaggressive and non-accusatory. Those factors switch us into defense mode, and nothing gets accomplished in that mindset.

I'll admit that while I was single, hearing people say they married their best friend made me cringe. My friends were the brothers on the job, and nothing, not even a wife, could break that bond. Well, it didn't take long after Leah and I married that I realized the big, huge, gigantic differences between work acquaintances and a best friend—my wife.

Leah's got my six, twenty-four hours a day, seven days a week. And part of that involves moving into each other's worlds to do activities the other may not prefer. Not because we want to, but because we love each other enough to do it anyway.

I used to do hundred-mile bike races, and I loved being in the saddle and on the road. Leah doesn't ride bikes, but she booked us a four-day trip biking from San Francisco to Sonoma Valley. She was sore. Very sore. But she came into my world because she knew I loved to bike. Along the same lines, Leah loves to go to movies. Being in a movie theater is one of my least favorite things to do, but I go because I'm getting to be part of her world and hang out with my best pal at the same time. It's a win-win situation.

You can and will disagree with your wife, but she is your most important ally, your constant backup, and forever your closest friend.

Domestic Safety

There's nothing like having a comfortable place to come home to. The job is tough, and there's comfort in knowing there's something safe on the other side of the fatality car crash or domestic dispute we're leaving from. Make the home a protected refuge for your family. Home is definitely where the heart is.

Deepest Needs

There sure seem to be a lot of needs when it comes to marriage and men and women. It could almost scare you into surrender. But these needs were planted deep in our hearts by the One who created us. It's done on purpose so we'll pursue someone other than ourselves. Namely, God and our spouse.

There are three very basic, but spiritual, needs. God designed us to share relationship with Him, and part of a loving, sacrificial union is the willingness to submit to the needs of each other. From the beginning, God sought us to rely upon Him to meet our most vital needs, so we could live a full, joy-centered life of worship and fellowship.

To realize this fulfilled life, we have a base need of love, security, and significance. Adam and Eve enjoyed the complete package, and in addition, they also enjoyed a seamless relationship with God. They didn't need a church, or prayers, or even the bible. Why? Because they were living the story with God every day in an up-close and personal relationship where there were open communications, friendship, and love.

God trusted man with the whole of His creation—earth. Man was placed there to tend and cultivate the land and every creature. He was given dominion over everything because God created him in His image and loved him enough to trust him.

The problem came for Adam and Eve as it comes for all of us in this life—sin. Once they chose rebellion over loving submission, they were no longer able to have the one-on-one relationship with the Creator. God didn't exile them from the garden for tasting the forbidden fruit. He sent them away to protect them from condemning themselves and all mankind to eternal death (separation from God).

Once they were exiled from paradise, they no longer had the direct connection to God to meet their needs for love, security, and significance. The outward source for satisfying their needs through God became an internalized failure to satisfy themselves apart from Him.

Jesus came as a bridge that leads us back into the garden of Eden. Because of this reconnection to the Father, we again have the opportunity to be filled by the Father instead of our worldly pursuits.

The problem we have is, after thousands of years of doing it our own way, we've become resistant to the notion of surrender. We don't live in a society that's known for surrendering anything. We want what we want, and we want to keep what's ours. Once we come into a posture of understanding that victory comes through surrendering to Jesus Christ, the potential for having the desire for love, significance, and security satisfied by God becomes a reality.

Are you in self-satisfaction mode? You love each other and you love your LEO job, and as long as you're happy doing what makes you happy, you're cool. Additionally, that paycheck from the agency, along with overtime, grant funding, and off-duty details helps you feel secure with a steady flow of cash. Our need for significance is bursting with pride as the uniform is adorned by that badge. LEO spouses may not wear the badge, but they carry the same pride for being a blue-line family.

By all appearances, it seems as though you've managed to satisfy your deepest needs for love, security, and significance, simply by working as a law enforcement officer. Well, you know we can't let that lie linger. Each one of those things can be wiped away in an instant. If you're putting your faith in law enforcement, then that becomes your god (lower case g). Once you've elevated something above God the Father, it also becomes idolatry.

Your reliance on the job to provide love, security, and significance will begin to decay. The love for the job will overshadow the love for each other. The security in salary and OT becomes a burden as expenses pile up and cost of living allowances don't. And your sense of significance because you carry the power of the shield will cause pride, which is akin to arrogance. What you both thought was saving and serving your needs, has, is, or will destroy what God intended for you.

Please don't allow fear of relying less on law enforcement and more on God to stop you from coming into a wonderful relationship with Him. Surrendering to God will indeed draw you both closer to Him and ultimately each other. God's purpose for your life is so important to understand. We all have one. His purpose for your life will fulfill the desires of your heart. Don't worry about opening yourself up to His will. He won't lead you to do something that He hasn't prepared you to do.

6

SILENCE, VIOLENCE AND RISK

"You're just like them."

Those words stung, but they were true. I'll never forget that night. My wife at the time hissed those words at me so our four-year-old son couldn't hear the latest in a series of escalating arguments.

I was an experienced undercover agent working with the DEA during the turbulent 1990s in a city rocked by violence and police corruption. New Orleans was not only the deadliest city in America, but the entire police department was being wiretapped by the FBI. Murder, drugs, bank robbery, and so many other violent felonies were about to be disclosed to the public when cops began going to prison.

Having my cover blown as a federal undercover agent working outside the lines of local jurisdiction should've been a red-light five-alarm wake-up call that danger was waiting to eat me alive. The drug dealers were dangerous, but the city cops were deadly. Instead, I'd never felt more alive.

I was in the thickest of the thick as we hunted down the most vicious criminals in the country. There was an attraction to that life that appealed to me. It was the ultimate adventure, but it was also the greatest threat to my marriage. I had become more ruthless and merciless than the vile predators we hunted.

Yet, there we sat. My innocent wife, who had only a year prior left her special-education teaching job to stay home with our son, was devastated. On the other hand, I was pumped up and anxious to get back to work. There was nothing I could say. I had changed, and like a giant, angry diesel locomotive, there was nothing either of us could've done without help to stop it. We didn't pursue counseling and the brothers at work were all too encouraging that I drop the marriage and start over. I'd become consumed with the sheepdog culture of violence, silence, and risk. We were divorced soon after.

Silence

I spent years traveling the country doing research for my doctoral dissertation about police culture. I spoke with hundreds of cops and spent countless hours hanging out listening to their conversations. What fascinated me then, and still today, were the similar patterns of behavior.

There is no single training academy for all law enforcement officers. There's not even a gold standard that dictates the way cops are trained or what they'll be taught in their training. Think about that for a moment. There are over 900,000 sworn law enforcement officers in America. Additionally, there are 17,985 independent law enforcement agencies ranging from college campus police to the FBI.

The only thread that ties us all together is no thread at all. It's culture, and the fraternity is united by the ethos of an imaginary thin blue line. Protecting the mystical veil of the profession is a code that every officer is expected to honor. It's not taught in any academy or regulation manual. It is the code of silence, and it goes for all cops on and off duty.

We'll state the obvious, but the code of silence doesn't help with an already growing lack of communications between you and your spouse. You must understand that there is a powerful force driving your personality and behavior. The academy and rookie season were ripe for shifting your worldview. As you progress through your career, you will also remain susceptible to change. But don't panic.

How do you prevent this shift in perspective from stealing away who you are as a person and driving a wedge between you and your wife without having to quit the job? Families play a key role in the overall health of every LEO. Family is an anchor in the storm, and a refuge from the relentless demands of an outside world. We begin separating ourselves from these familial ties as we slide deeper into the isolated culture of our agency.

Spouses have a cross to carry by the very nature of their LEO relationship, but in addition to the stress and worry, we must be vigilant for signs of social and emotional detachment. The more we value our brothers in blue, the less attached we are to our wives. Open communication with your spouse will alert you to the process of detaching from them.

Violence

"Certainly there is no hunting like the hunting of man, and those who have hunted armed men long enough and liked it, never really care for anything else thereafter."
Ernest Hemingway

I'd been on the job about seven years before my first wife and I sat in that back bedroom to have the final talk. It was about six years too late. I was so deeply embedded in the cop culture that neither one of us knew how to escape.

LEOs begin to change from day one in the basic training academy. It's designed to take away the civilian, and replace it with a like-thinking replica of the last cadet who graduated. It's called homogeneity, and it's vital that we all come from the same cloth to ensure compliance. Even if it means destruction in our personal life.

Sameness means safety in policing. Once you graduate and are on your way into a field training program, you're bombarded with pressure to fit within a mold to get along. Occupational socialization is the term, but it's no more than learning the flow of the job, and not swimming against it no matter what. The most important goal of the LEO is to fit in.

Ever heard, "Forget that junk they taught you in the academy. This is where you learn to be a real cop." Yeah, we all got that talk. It was to ensure you molded into the way they thought and behaved.

One of the ways LEOs gain acceptance from our new peers is through violence. The cold hard truth is that police are the state's arm of violence. When the legislature creates laws, it is the job of law enforcement to enforce those laws. Now by violence, there are several levels that you are familiar with referred to as the use of force continuum. From someone threatening to call the cops, to a LEO shooting a suspect, is all considered "violence" because it's force applied. Either actual or perceptual, it's the state's way of making sure people comply with the laws they enact.

This violence becomes a rite of passage into the cop culture. The more violence you apply, the more respected you are among your peers. It's not difficult for LEOs to begin identifying with their ability and willingness to apply the various levels of violence. Some may take the power of authority in stopping cars for traffic tickets, while others pride themselves in the fights and suspects apprehended.

The threat to you begins when the lines blur and violence comes home through bragging, stress from having committed the violence, harsh language, or the use of violence to control the home life like it's used to control the public.

We shared the data from the national study of domestic violence (DV) committed by police on their families. The numbers are disturbing but dramatically under-represented because cops keep things in-house when offenses are committed and covered up by brother officers, or just never reported.

Some of the reasons that make LEO-initiated DV different from other victims is that the LEO abuser:

Has a gun.

Knows the locations of the battered women's shelters.

Knows how to operate within the system to avoid consequences and even shift blame to the victim.

Is usually friends or close work associates with officers who would respond to handle the complaint.

Agencies go to great lengths to cover incidents of reported DV. This often gives the LEO a false sense of empowerment in believing dominant behavior at home is acceptable. It is not. We don't condone this at all, but it is a reality of life behind the thin blue line, and an even more important reason that both of you invest in your marriage.

Risk

There's a belief among LEOs that we cannot live the "white picket fence" life. I was guilty of saying that until I began to understand why we think we can't exist in a normal, drama-free off-duty life. Without tethers to the outside world, all we know is what we know. If that is the rough and hard life of policing, then that is what we become. Kinda like "You are what you eat."

Familial, social, religious, and civic anchors are the first to be sliced away once we slip deeper into the blue culture. But it's these very tethers that keep us grounded and safely behind that white picket fence. This is where your spouse must play detective. Making a mental note of the "old" activities you both used to participate in, versus those you now avoid in exchange for hanging out with your new buds from shift is vital to early detection in a change of personal values. One of the first to go is spending time with non-LEO friends and couples. While your wife is still attached to them, you no longer feel they understand you or that they judge you because of the badge, so you eliminate them from your life. Your wife suffers more because the decision wasn't hers.

Sure, everyone wants to fit in and get to know their co-workers, but when we cloak ourselves in nothing but work and co-workers, it's time to remind ourselves where work falls on the list of priorities. Trust me, if not done early and often, you will lose yourself to the fraternity.

Without grounding, your identity becomes rooted in that of those you identify with. The first problem is that while we pray God blesses all cops, none of them are Jesus Christ. Your identity should always mirror that of Christ. When that is the priority, most other problems of shady influences will take care of themselves.

No one ever improved their career by improving their tolerance to alcohol. It's tough being a light in the culture of dark blue. My first several years on the job, I carried my bible to the academy, in my patrol cruiser, and into my drug task force commander's office. I was ridiculed and excluded from most of the after-hours choir practices.

It wasn't until I began to take the risk of hanging with the guys after shift, or making a big arrest and celebrating with the boys and beer, that life began to change for the worse. Again, this was almost thirty years ago, and there was no one, and I mean no one, to tell me I could do better.

Risk is part of our profession. Oftentimes, we place ourselves in more risk than is necessary for the sake of a rookie mistake that allows adrenaline to overcome common sense, or just to feel alive. Why? Because we see what's behind that white picket fence as domestic, average, and boring.

The white picket fence that we dread is actually a boundary. We'll cover the importance of boundaries later, but for now, it's important to know boundaries do exist and they are not for keeping the fun and excitement out of your marriage. They are there to protect what is most important. Both of you should identify your priorities, and guard them within your marriage's fence.

Instability

The banging on the window outside of my young son's bedroom stirred me. I'd fallen asleep by his side waiting for him to doze off, and I reached for a weapon that wasn't there. I hurried back to my room and slipped my hand inside the nightstand to remove my weapon. I held the weapon at ready gun, and peeked through the gap in the curtains. It was one of my rookie officers.

Because we're cops, that scenario wasn't odd. Most people would find that strange that it wasn't odd. I waved him to the front door where I saw his marked cruiser in the driveway with every LED light flashing. My neighbors must've loved that scene at three in the morning. Dispatch had repeatedly called my cell, and the rookie had knocked on the door, but I was exhausted and dead to the world.

They needed to know I was alive, and had protection sent to each of my commanders' homes to check on them as well. Earlier in the night, a group of armed thugs broke into the home of one of my officers and tried to assassinate him and his family. A brief exchange of shots fired and a foot chase resulted in the bad guys getting away, and my agency was put on high alert.

So there I was, requested to jump into chief mode while my eight-year-old son with Down syndrome slept. And Leah was out of town for work. How many other professions face that scenario?

Just like you, we've been interrupted from birthdays, holidays, and just wanting to do nothing for days because the job needed us right then and there. I can't imagine too many other families that even know what a Go-Bag is.

The irony is, while we pre-plan, plan, and re-plan to make sure we're operationally ready, the preparation creates a dynamic of disengagement within the marriage. Back in the day, I was proud to wear my beeper (I'm dating myself). But it was a constant reminder to everyone that I was subject to callouts at any time. Today, smart phones are such an integral part of our lives that there's no distinction between a friendly social media post and a SWAT hostage activation.

The point is, the LEO's life is fraught with instability. While the time spent behind the badge is exciting for us, the reality is, your wife is abandoned once again at the family vacation, or tucking the kids into bed and sticking a romantic supper back in the fridge. Instability is an enemy to intimacy.

LEO marriages are tough, but the truth is, so is every other marriage. Data for Americans shows that first marriages fail 50 percent of the time. Giving it the old second try will end up in divorce court 63 percent of the time, but by the third marriage we know better, right? Nope, those marriages fail 74 percent of the time.

Think there's instability in marriage? Good, because there is. Now remember, these statistics are not specific to LEO marriages. This is a snapshot of the general public to include LEOs and the folks who have steady nine-to-five jobs and weekends off without bullets flying and felons swinging at your face.

I always hesitate to share any attempt at quoting LEO divorce rates because reports are all over the place. Although divorce and remarriage wasn't the focus of a research project I conducted, it was a question asked to over two hundred officers. The results showed LEO marriages failing about 80 percent of the time.

So why even try? You know, that's a great question, and without the solid foundation of biblical principles, that question would be profound. But the truth is, we were created to enjoy relationships—particularly marriage. God's relationship with us is the original marriage covenant model and is the reason why it's replicated between a man and a woman.

The reality is, the marriage model has suffered the difficulties of humanity just as any institution relying on two people's ability to maintain a similar pace, commitment, and effort might. We're human, and life sometimes gets in the way. For the LEO couple, the instability of the job adds to the degree of difficulty. Let's take a look at some of the culprits.

Perception

While this section is titled Perception, the truth is, each of these areas have a high potential for becoming reality.

Risk of On-Duty Death

Leah has more than once dropped a truth bomb among friends about her fears of my being killed at work. It can be a buzzkill, but the truth is, before I retired it was a worry for her. Although we LEOs grow to accept line-of-duty deaths as part of the profession, it's not a natural inclination. The average life expectancy in the United States for males is 76.3 years, while females fare better at 84.72 years of age. LEOs at twenty-one years old and up understand that the average is not a luxury they may come to know. That's not healthy for a marriage, but it's one of the more unstable costs of doing the job.

Research shows that LEOs have an elevated risk of death relative to the general population and for several specific causes. Life expectancy is significantly lower than the general public, and death is more pronounced in younger age categories. The years of potential life lost for police officers is twenty-one times larger than that of the general population. Some of the reasons for this diminished life expectancy include stress, shift work, obesity, hazardous environmental work exposures, and cumulative PTSD.

Even soldiers in combat who understand death is a risk, are only under those extreme high-threat conditions for a defined period of deployment in foreign lands. For LEOs, it's a persistent potential for as long as the career lasts, and it occurs in the same communities within which we live.

Shifting Worldview

Cultural assimilation is a fancy pants way of saying, "fitting in." I was so optimistic and naïve when I began the basic training academy. That would change immediately. It was both a necessity for gaining street smarts, and adopting a work mindset that meshed with my peers.

Most, if not all LEOs, will experience this view shift. It doesn't matter if you served in the military first, or played cop-themed video games your entire life. There's nothing to prepare you for police basic training. The way you see the world will change with a healthy dose of skepticism. But that skepticism will keep you alive. It can also callous a heart toward marriage.

For the spouse, they're often left wondering what happened to the person they married. The shift is gradual enough over time so that you don't recognize it. But your spouse will. This is why communication is so vital, and where understanding can save a marriage. There's no place for defensiveness in this conversation.

Life in the Fishbowl

It's one thing to be well known in your community, but it's completely different when your notoriety comes with mixed feelings of animosity, admiration, and unrealistic expectations. Once you pin that badge on, the position within the community changes.

Not only is your life examined through the clouded waters of the social fishbowl, but so is your family. Most civilians have the opportunity to manage public images via social media, but as a LEO, there is zero control over what's printed, posted, or alleged against you. LEOs are no longer the fish, but the chum for others to attack you, your agency, and the national profession of law enforcement.

Why? Because LEOs are seen as the moral entrepreneurs, and by gosh, if we're going to uphold that law, then we better live by the letter of it. Leah and I couldn't eat out at local restaurants without being approached with kindness from most, but condemnation from some. While kids shaking your hand at the local burger joint can be fun, it's another reminder that the life we live is not our own. Although we might be better adapted to the constant public onslaught, our spouse didn't sign up for the peering eyes of social assessment.

Closed Fraternity

While friendships and a tight working environment might be good things, the LEO culture can quickly slide off the rails and into a gulch of self-serving protection of the agency, the squad, and each other. This closed-wall environment often means wives find themselves on the outside with no understanding of why or what caused the separation.

This circling of the wagons is a behavioral pattern that easily extends into your marriage when times come where an apology or confession would go a long way. Instead, we learn to protect ourselves by closing ranks and circling the wagons. You must be aware of this as it'll show itself through regular communications with your spouse. Simple questions that lead to long explanations are a first clue that you are no longer comfortable with transparent conversation. This isn't the time for you to barricade. Honest communication is the key.

Shift Work and Callouts

I started my career working the twelve-hour tours. The constant rotation from day shift to night shift has been shown to cause significant issues with fatigue, performance, and overall safety when LEOs are operating on the ragged edge.

I've read studies that also show there are no harmful effects, but what I've yet to see is research that focuses on the family. I know firsthand, just as you do, that when we're on rotating shifts—and your spouse either stays at home, or works a more traditional workweek—it causes real-life problems.

In addition to the instability of shifting shifts, callouts are also a destabilizing factor that LEO couples are forced to contend with. While you may be off to an unknown adventure or emergency response, it's your abandoned wife who's left to care for the kids, honor the RSVP at events, meet teachers, and make doctor's appointments. It becomes a bit overwhelming.

Missed Connections

Sex

Two important needs in any marriage are sex and communication. God created sex, but the world acts like the devil owns it. It's critical that we take it back and set it squarely in the middle of our marriages. When you find validation through work, you'll notice your spouse isn't the intimate partner they once were. Don't be afraid to initiate sex and restore sex as a priority in marriage.

Sex is God's covenant seal between husband and wife. When Genesis 2:24 says that the man and his wife become one flesh, that is exactly what we're talking about—sex. Yes, sex is that important in a marriage. This is our time to share ourselves with our spouse, and only our spouse.

Therefore a man shall leave his father and his mother and hold fast to his wife, and they shall become one flesh.
Genesis 2:24

Communication

The struggles for LEO couples come when each person is busy with their own careers, schedules, and friends. Because the LEO culture is rooted in silence and isolation, it causes a lack of attention and intimacy between you and your spouse. This, of course, also breaks the flow that usually leads to intimacy and/or sex. Also, invest in time with your spouse that doesn't always mean sex. Nonsexual, intimate contact goes a long way toward building a deep connection.

Intimacy is also shown through active listening and engaged communication. Unfortunately, this isn't a characteristic associated with the LEO culture. We can spend hours talking to other LEOs about cases, promotions, assignments, and the stress of inter-office politics, but we won't invest the same amount of time talking with our spouse unless it's about police work.

What happens is that when men who speak the language of respect and women who speak the language of security begin to feel that neither are getting the type of communication they need, silence usually follows. We can tell you that silence is a marriage killer. Open up and always be vulnerable (naked) to each other.

Fighting Fair

Finally, please practice speaking with kindness to each other. Leah and I call it "Fighting Fair." Sure, I can out argue her and intimidate her into almost any decision I want through pure force of will and stubbornness. But is that how God wants us to care for our spouse?

Leah is a true creative spirit. Her mind functions very differently from my concrete way of seeing things. She'll get the inspiration to rearrange or completely redesign a room in our home. When she tries to share her vision, I've been known to shoot it down before she ever gets out more than a paragraph. It wounds her to the core because creativity is her heart's way of expressing herself, and it's her way of showing the family love through design and beauty.

What I perceive in her sharing a vision for interior design is that she disrespects my wish for saving money because I know it's going to cost more than a can of paint. I allow my insecurity to drive what should be an open conversation about what each of us want out of a space in the house.

In those moments, I don't fight fair. And like most cops, we're well versed in verbal jousting. This means we can out argue, manipulate, or flatly shut down a conversation. If I'm not mindful, I'll do that to my beloved. Even after an apology and asking for forgiveness, I know her sweet spirit still carries around the scar.

God says the tongue holds the power of death and life. There's also no coincidence that the very next verse in Proverbs 18 talks about how a man who finds a wife finds a good thing and a blessing from God. This association is coupled together to illustrate how important it is for us to speak power over and into each other's lives.

It's also a reminder to us that we've been blessed with a wonderful gift from God in our spouse. Please remember that the way we treat the gift reflects on how we feel about the gift giver. By caring for our spouse, we honor God.

> *Death and life are in the power of the tongue,*
> *and those who love it will eat its fruits.*
> *He who finds a wife finds a good thing*
> *and obtains favor from the Lord.*
> *Proverbs 18:21–22*

Solid Foundation

Leah and I don't know where you and your wife are in terms of your walk of faith. We don't want to make assumptions, because ultimately, that relationship is between you and God. It's important to rely on the only complete source of information for building a rock-solid relationship.

God's Word provides both spiritual and practical advice for couples who have shared sacred vows with each other. Simply attending church will no more save your marriage than sitting in a garage will make you a car. Using these bible-based marriage principles will lead you into a deeper understanding and relational intimacy.

How do we strengthen the foundations of instability in LEO marriages? By building it on the solid rock of Christ, and not the shifting sands of this world. Take a moment and read this passage from Matthew 7.

Therefore everyone who hears these words of mine and puts them into practice is like a wise man who built his house on the rock. The rain came down, the streams rose, and the winds blew and beat against that house; yet it did not fall, because it had its foundation on the rock. But everyone who hears these words of mine and does not put them into practice is like a foolish man who built his house on sand. The rain came down, the streams rose, and the winds blew and beat against that house, and it fell with a great crash."
Matthew 7:24–27

This verse applies to everything in life. Please allow these simple words to speak to you both. Try substituting the word *house* with *marriage*. Switch out rain, floods and winds for three things that are attacking your marriage right now.

When we personalize it to our story, it hits home. Jesus is not talking about a house; He's talking about you.

This verse as applied to my life would've looked like this at one point:

Everyone then who hears these words of mine and does them will be like a wise LEO couple who built their marriage on the rock (Christ). And the job stresses fell, and the sexual temptations came, and the threat of divorce blew and beat on our marriage, but it did not fall, because it had been founded on the rock (Jesus).

I'm willing to bet this adapted version reflects many of your own experiences. If not, just add your life story into God's Word and see how it speaks to you. The important message is that we will fail if we depend only on ourselves. We do not have the power to thrive absent of God in an environment created by Him. On the other hand, we will be blessed beyond belief once we stand within His marriage covenant.

Facing the facts while growing your LEO marriage will help you both avoid many of these instability problems. If you're already deep into your relationship and are looking for help, then knowing what the issues are will help you identify them, discuss them, and overcome them. It's never too late to get it right.

7

INFIDELITY

Years ago I had an officer come into my office with a look of defeat and confusion. He huffed out a big gulp of air before his meaty hands began scrubbing at his ruddy face. I was concerned as a red flush crept up beneath his uniform shirt collar until his entire big bald head was a bright crimson blush.

"Chief, why do cops cheat?"

I was caught off guard at the cavalier nature of the question from someone who I knew was on his third marriage.

"It's just part of cop culture," I said.

He said thanks and walked out. I returned to my work with an emptiness for not really having a depth of consideration to respond accurately. I knew there was more than blaming it on some informal group dynamic, so I began to dig deeper for answers.

My first shove of the shovel in unearthing answers was to examine my own life. Infidelity wasn't something I considered during the twenty years of being single (post-divorced), but the truth was, even when I tried to enter into committed relationships, I cheated. Exposure wasn't the reason those relationships ended, but it might as well have been. In hindsight, it was a combination of unmet expectations, as well as carrying personal pain amplified by the job.

But still, why do LEOs cheat?

Infidelity is a painful and complex topic, but we'd be derelict in our duties if we didn't discuss why it occurs and ways to prevent it from destroying marriages. And while the majority of my understanding focuses on why male LEOs cheat, we don't want to imply that female LEOs are incapable of straying either.

One day I was discussing a potential research project, and a female co-worker suggested I examine why married female basic academy cadets cheat or have sex with an instructor or another cadet. Stunned, I said no way. She smiled and admitted she'd had an affair, and then she pointed to three other female officers who I'd worked closely with and respected as personal friends. They all nodded that they too had an affair while attending their basic training academy.

So, to be fair, there's no discrimination against the guys or girls on this subject. It doesn't make it right, but it does make it a reality that extends beyond gender.

Placating

The first time I learned that infidelity wasn't only a sexual or moral issue, I scoffed. How could running around on your wife not involve wandering sexual desires, or that your morals left something to be desired? The notion that all guys were horndogs chasing tail because they have a healthy sex drive is a lie we guys tell each other because we're either too ashamed to admit the truth, or we simply don't know why we do it. The boys will be boys alibi hurts everyone.

The reality in most, but not all cases of sexual addiction or obsession concerning infidelity is about placating our feelings of pain, shame, and guilt. Admitting we need help is not a cultural option because we refuse to be seen as weak. Needing to talk to someone or confide in another that we are hurt is something strictly prohibited. Sex is a common way we try dealing with what ails us. It gives us a temporary sense of the power, control, and intimacy (false) that we may lack or long for. You suck it up and deal with it in your own silence. And then you wait for it to go away.

Time does not heal wounds. It only makes them worse!

Men silently suffer for decades, and we think it's noble to go to our grave with the secrets buried along with us. The problem is, your suffering affects everyone, all of the time. Whether we know it or even realize it, it's got us by the cojones and is destructively controlling us.

Men often turn to sex to ease that hurt. We placate the feelings of inadequacy through physical, virtual, or fantasy affairs. While it would seem the logical choice is to confide in your spouse and seek her loving, physical, emotional, and spiritual care, it would require us to become vulnerable. Because we speak the language of respect, to show or tell our wife that we're vulnerable goes against the very heart of how we communicate. It also jeopardizes our need to be revered as the protector and warrior.

The impersonal attachment to porn, sexting, or social media hookups allows us to apply a temporary ointment or bandage to what deeply haunts us. It also allows us to maintain the façade of being in control of our feelings if only for a little while, or at least until the suffering returns.

These dark feelings come from many sources, but because we fail to talk about it with our spouses, we don't know how to process it. We think that being hard and tough is the way to cover it up and still live the heroic blue line lifestyle. On average, fathers don't teach their sons how to be real men. All my dad taught me was how to be tough. Why tough? Because he usually hurt me, and the only way to get through my childhood was to become tough. Did it cause problems? Yep.

When all we know is what we know, I imitated his dominating, chauvinistic ways. My mother was a sweet woman, but beneath his thumb she was no more than a child in our home. When I slip up and command Leah to do something, I immediately hear my dad saying the very same things to my mom. It hurt me as a child, and it hurts me as Leah's husband to know that those old tendencies still reside in my nature.

What we want you to know is that Leah and I understand what you're going through. You spend lots of time away from your spouse while you're on duty, in court, or training. And it's tough. But when the temptation of infidelity refuses to give you a break, it's time to confide to your spouse with the truth of how you feel and what it is that you need to get through the dark season.

It's Not Harmless Fun

Infidelity has been normalized in cop culture because it's so pervasive. All because "everybody is doing it" doesn't make it right. Marital purity is serious business. The disciple James makes it very clear that temptation results from man's lure of desire. Giving in to that desire causes man to sin. The result of that sin is death.

But each person is tempted when he is lured and enticed by his own desire. Then desire when it has conceived gives birth to sin, and sin when it is fully grown brings forth death.
James 1:14–15

Will sexual sin kill you? Well, we guess it depends on the circumstances, depending on if your wife is holding a weapon when she catches you. Notice I say when she catches you. Your wife is God's precious daughter. Do you really think He's going to let you get away with hurting her?

The death that James talks about comes in the form of separation from God, loss of your wife, family, career, reputation, sense of self, and the many other tangible wages of sin.

Need more convincing? Check out what the apostle Paul says about our lame excuse as "boys being boys."

Flee from sexual immorality. Every other sin a person commits is outside the body, but the sexually immoral person sins against his own body.
1 Corinthians 6:18

Paul doesn't wink and warn to stay away, or flirt, or just take one peek. He says to flee. Paul warns that sexual sin is the only act where man sins against his own body. Sexual sin is so serious that it has been singled out by God. Every time two people have intercourse, they leave an imprint on each other. By engaging in an affair, the husband now attaches that illegitimate imprint of his mistress on to his beloved wife. Is that fair to her?

Let's wrap this section up with Proverbs. It always gets straight to the point.

He who commits adultery lacks sense; he who does it destroys himself.
He will get wounds and dishonor, and his disgrace will not be wiped
away.
Proverbs 6:32–33

Willing to Look?

Do you or your wife have an issue with sexual addiction that promotes infidelity? Most people scatter when the topic is brought up in public, or even in the church. Just the mention conjures up images of seedy alleyways or trench-coat creepers offering candy for van rides. Men are quick to say they're not addicted to porn or that they tossed their stash of nudie mags once the kids were born.

Would you both be willing to take a quick test? The sexual addiction screening test is confidential, free, and no one's business. If you have the slightest inclination that you or your LEO's actions are damaging, or that they try to stop but usually keep slipping, or the pain, guilt, or shame continue to grind away, please take a moment to check this out.

Try it out by clicking here, or visiting https://conquerseries.com/sast/

Dark Secrets

The darkness of sexual sin will never lead to healing. Satan uses the powerful ruse of secrets to bind men to the chains of hell. LEOs take stock in each other's ability to maintain confidentiality. Being trustworthy and loyal are characteristics we seek and value. But at what costs?

Men even buy into the belief that the other woman is trustworthy, and she understands us much better than our wife does. How can she not care? After all, we've confided our past hurts, and complained about our job, our supervisor, and our wife to her, and she still wants to sleep together. Surely, mistresses understand men better, and can be trusted with anything. And surely, they would never do anything to ruin a good thing by letting hints slip to your wife so they could become the next Mrs. fill in the blank.

Adultery is a baited hook. Men don't see the slimy worm on the barbed tip. They see the desirable allure of an easy escape from their past hurts and current problems. That first bite seals the deal. A man is now trapped by whether his mistress decides to tell his wife or not. For LEOs who value their alpha ability to control dangerous scenarios and violent criminals, they've just surrendered all control of their very own life to a stranger for anonymous sex.

The man has surrendered the entirety of his life to someone he may have just met on a call for service, at the gym, or online. Guess what? Sometimes men are in such deep pain that they don't even care about getting busted. They see themselves as unworthy of having a happy, loving wife and family.

Men in agony don't see consequences. If they get busted for cheating, then divorce is not seen as a consequence, but as an opportunity for starting over. Not healing the problem that is causing the destructive behavior locks them into a dangerous cycle.

Binge-Purge Cycle

People don't have the natural ability to simply say, "I'll quit." It's deeper than willpower or surface-level decision-making. This isn't like losing weight or going to the gym before summer starts. The root cause may lie buried in layers as far back as childhood, or as recent as last month. Either way, it requires more than a cursory assurance to "behave."

Men who cheat exist in a vicious cycle known as Binge-Purge. There may be days, weeks, or even years between episodes of infidelity, but until the pain, secrets, and sin are confessed, men will continue to churn in that sexual storm. For the LEO whose reputation means more than truth's reality, making himself vulnerable is a toxic idea.

Some men go years without clicking that website link late at night, but once the need becomes too strong, he finds himself consuming porn on the computer for hours or days until he's either confronted or expended by guilt. He'll make a sincere pledge to never do it again, but without healing, he'll be back because apologies are only as effective as the next soul-splitting pain attack and all-night click-baiting of deviant URL searches. It's an unrelenting cycle where the desperation to ease the hurt begins to cause pain through guilt greater than the initial wound.

Healing Light

While pornography was the example used above, this is equally applied to adultery, flirtations, and social media communications. It all goes back to darkness in our lives and a desperate desire to feel in control of something or someone. Keeping truth in the dark, keeping actions in secret, and keeping freedom from sexual bondage will not heal anything.

The only way to heal is to bring it into the light. I'm going to say this, and I know the risk of losing you, but we men need help. It's foolish to think it can be handled without it. I love this quote:

"We can't solve problems by using the same kind of thinking we used when we created them."
Albert Einstein

LEOs need accountability partners. Other men who've been through it and not only weathered the storms, but learned to construct barriers and protections from the threats and dangers. Many churches offer small groups or online resources to provide unwilling egos with mentors to help other men who struggle to weather the storms.

Iron sharpens iron, and one man sharpens another.
Proverbs 27:17

God equates light with goodness and healing. Confession, repentance, and consistent sincere attention will help everyone find light, forgiveness, and God's grace. If you are struggling to deal with your darkness, now is the time to find help. Men can recover from sexual sin. We can even repair the destruction caused to our wife and family, but that takes effort. Are you willing to make that effort? I can tell you from personal experience, no one can want it more for you than you want it for yourself.

We Can / We Can't

I know what you're thinking. This isn't us. I'm not messing around with another woman. Our intention isn't to make you paranoid, but it is to make you aware that the high majority of LEOs are struggling with some form of need or temptation.

Maybe it was from responding to a fatal car crash, or maybe it's just that your supervisor is a jerk, or the fact that women give you attention when you're in uniform. No matter the source, it's vital that your wife has your back. Of course that requires you to openly communicate with her about everything that might be going on. We are talking about bulletproofing your marriage, and not stroking an ego.

Most cops I know never discussed marital purity. It was a joke to even talk about being faithful. It might just be locker room talk, but if it's being said, it's being fed. Sexual temptation is one of the greatest threats to a LEO's career.

There's a warning I was given on my first day on the job by a senior officer who I still value today. I'll keep it appropriate for this book, but you understand: "Your badge will get you women, but women will get your badge."

Now, since I'm not lecturing a police academy class of rookie cadets, I'll expand this advice. Whatever their realm may be—social media, website pornography, office romance, or the nightclubs—the same principle applies.

The secrets of sexual sin lock men down into a bondage they cannot easily escape. Satan has got them by the balls, and unless they seek the help to bring past pain and current sin to healing light, you and your wife will lose more than you can ever imagine. Men can do better, but we can't do it on our own.

Epidemic Infidelity

Okay, now the natural, practical side of why infidelity reigns unchecked for LEOs. Do you recall when we said that LEO marriages were special? Well, they are. And as any marriage should be treated as special, yours takes on a context that no other can match. But when it comes to infidelity, the LEO behavior falls in line with several cross-cultural dynamics that we'd bet no one told you about before you said, "I do."

Jobs that involve long shifts and time away from home with an anonymity while working opens the LEO up to the constant risk of opportunity. Add to it the types of vulnerable people LEOs often come into contact with, and you're starting to paint a picture that would match several other professions such as nurses, truckers, soldiers, firefighters, and salesmen, just to name a few.

Policing in and of itself doesn't cause anyone to cheat. If the LEO is looking to cheat, they are placed in an environment where accountability is low, temptation is constant, and the authority of the uniform, the badge, and weapon makes the casual sex easy, then they will have zero problem accomplishing their mission.

It's the officers caught in the middle that suffer because of the environment. They find themselves without peers who openly promote marriage or purity. Instead, the majority of co-workers have been married several times, actively cheat on their spouse, and do so knowing that it gains them social points among the other cops. The need to fit in causes a complex situation for the LEO who wants to be faithful, but doesn't want to become a work outcast.

I worked with an undercover agent for years who to this day remains married to his first wife. He was a natural born cop with incredible street instincts and a nose for sniffing out dope, no matter how well the bad guy tried to hide it. He also had a penchant for sleeping with every woman who walked his way.

I recall asking him one night how he managed to get away with sleeping with women from his very own agency, as well as the numerous one-night stands while out of town on assignment or training. He laughed proudly and said that the key was to have sex with his wife as soon as he got home. That way she'd never suspect him of sleeping around while out of town.

He knew about it, I knew about it, and I'd guess about fifty or so other cops have known about it over the twenty-five plus years that he and his wife have been married. He knew there was no need to worry about his brothers ratting him out because the married ones were doing the same thing they'd learned from him.

What pushes these LEOs over to the dark side of infidelity isn't the temptation of easy sex at work. It's issues associated with family conflicts, unmet expectations from the spouse, dissatisfaction with their job, or low self-esteem.

For the LEO's spouse, they are always on call as a marriage detective. Did you know if a wife suspects her husband is cheating, she's right 85 percent of the time? A woman knows when she doesn't have intimacy (physical or emotional) with her husband, or when she's treated as an afterthought.

I didn't want my wife getting into my business. I remember telling her once that I had a right to my privacy. What I was really saying was that my privacy protected my sin from her. Leah wasn't stupid. She dug, pushed, scratched, and fought to protect our marriage.

Trust me, you might not be happy that your wife showed up at the bar to drag you home, but you'll thank her later.

There's something I tell my brothers in blue when they come to see me after they're already in crisis. "If you want to keep your badge, your wife, and your dignity, keep your pants zipped." It usually makes them mad, but if it wasn't the truth, they wouldn't be in crisis. These aren't harmless junior high crushes. Your marriage is in a fishbowl so everyone can see. If you think no one knows, then you have to shake that fishbowl up a bit and become aware that someone is always watching and just dying to bust your bubble the same way you bust speeders.

Here's a great reference from our friend, Pastor Dave Willis. He and his lovely wife, Ashley, have helped so many marriages by sharing this simple advice. We apply it to our marriage, and we know it will help yours.

Seven Rules Guaranteed to Prevent Infidelity

1. Never meet alone with a woman other than your wife.
2. When you send text messages to another woman (other than your mom), include your wife on the text.
3. Share ALL passwords. "In marriage, secrets are as dangerous as lies."
4. Don't watch porn or sexually explicit content.
5. Give "side" hugs to other women.
6. Don't engage in ongoing dialogue with women on social media.
7. Make time together with your wife a priority.

8

BLENDED FAMILY

Foundations for Blending Families

Leah and I are aware that no resource for marriage would be complete without a section dedicated to blended families. We host a small group at our home twice a month for married couples, and what we've learned is that the term blended family is so much more expansive than the traditional definition of two people marrying with kids from a previous relationship.

The nontraditional nuclear family is almost a thing of the past once we consider how personal dynamics affect a marriage. There's your traditional blended family, consisting of two people marrying and combining their kids from another relationship. Then there are those who have kids who have recently married, and now sons- and daughters-in-law become a type of blended family as you're facing new dynamics. Then there's boomerang kids, adoptions, fostering, elderly relatives moving in, and the many other potentials for doing life outside of the tidy box once described as *marriage*. It's a whole new world for blended families.

While we wish it wasn't such a necessity, the reality is law enforcement families are very nontraditional. The divorce rate is so high, and the culture so enclosed, that it's not uncommon for cops to marry other cops, or another cop's spouse after a divorce. We see it all the time.

We always make it a point to emphasize that we are pro-marriage. We love to see those "first-timers" who met and married and got it right the first time. If your marriage is in jeopardy, we pray you'll stay in the fight and begin to place your focus on the Rock of Jesus Christ. Divorce is hell, and benefits no one but the attorneys.

Now that we've got our disclaimer out of the way, let's get into the reality of cops and blended families. The marriage-go-round among LEOs is a culturally incestuous anomaly. But whether LEOs marry someone from inside the circle, or someone from another planet, the blue fraternity priority kicks in, and blending families becomes an entirely different challenge for LEO marriages to overcome.

There is no data on law enforcement blended families and divorces. The national average shows that 50 percent of the entire US population consists of blended families. Of those remarried couples, they will divorce over 60 percent of the time, unless they bring kids along with them into that second marriage. Although we might love those little buggers, blended families fail 70 percent of the time thanks to the stresses of raising other people's children.

Now, take into account how much more difficult law enforcement is on the marriage and family. Even without empirical data, you know the chances of a remarriage and blended family being successful are slim. So why do we do it? Most people cite hope as a main reason they retake the plunge despite the odds.

Leah and I want to give you something that most people don't have going into a blended family. We want to give you hope through truth. It's tough and although we approached blending families with a cautious eye and lots of research, making this life together almost didn't happen.

I'm going to throw another truth bomb at you in hopes you'll see that when Leah and I say we should never have made it, you will understand the severity of the odds we beat. Yes, I say beat and not beating, because we claim victory over the destruction of divorce. We beat the odds and so can you.

We all know the success rate statistics of first, second, and third marriages. Estimates of law enforcement divorces run between 70–80 percent. Now recall that we just showed blended families fail 60 percent of the time, and with kids it jumps to 70 percent.

Consider that I'd been divorced twice, and Leah divorced once. I'm a cop, and she'd never had anyone close to her who wore a badge. We've got seven kids between us in this blended adventure. We also have a special needs child. Marriages with special needs children fail 80 percent of the time.

I'm no mathematician, but we didn't stand a snowball's chance in hades with those odds stacked against us. Not to mention that I carried around so much baggage after twenty-five years in policing, I wasn't a good catch for anyone. Leah only came to understand the effect the job had on me after my retirement as I began to crumble beneath PTSD, addiction, and a life of past abuse that surfaced once the façade's glue came undone.

When Leah and I began to move toward marriage, we decided it was the right time to introduce our children into our relationship. She brought four young kids into the mix. It wasn't a surprise, as we'd been up front from the very beginning, and neither of us would've continued to flirt with the idea of advancing the relationship unless the other fully accepted the "kids factor."

I love kids, but I really love my own. To say I immediately welcomed and loved hers as my own would not be telling you the truth. Two of the four were little more than babies. They youngest had just finished potty training. I was forty-eight years old at the time, and they were introduced to me in a full-blown chief-of-police uniform, surrounded by other officers in full cop mode. I would have to imagine it was a bit intimidating, if not frightening.

That first, long weekend saw many crying fits, hiding, and running through other parts of the house to avoid me, and they desperately sought the comfort from other siblings and their mom. Leah and I didn't panic or call it a failure. We remained patient and united. What followed were months spent drawing boundaries and erasing battle lines; losing and gaining trust; high-fiving and avoiding confrontation.

Honestly, I wasn't doing well in the compassion department where little kids were concerned. I was used to Max knowing when I was kidding around. I can be intimidating, and the truth is, I can also be overbearing. I'd lived alone for almost twenty years. I liked things my way.

Showing emotion wasn't something I was allowed to express growing up under a dominant father. So naturally, I wasn't skilled or comfortable with their emotional outbursts. My standard response was usually to tell them to stop it. Sometimes it worked, other times they cried more.

I was at a point of telling Leah I couldn't take their crying anymore. I'd grown up fighting my siblings like animals. I played rough sports, I liked to fight, and my career was spent in the most violent assignments. So when presented with two young boys who preferred video games to footballs, I was at my wits' end.

One morning I prayed that God would show me how to be a compassionate father for them, and not a task-driven chief of police. I felt the chains of uncertainty fall from me. I was shown that I held fear that by showing love to these boys, that my love for my own boys would be chipped away.

I saw that you cannot run out of giving love. The more you give, the more you have to give. It's like Jesus and the five loaves of bread and fish. Love is unconditional, so the supply is unending. It wasn't a matter of sharing a certain measure of love, but the expanding of my capacity to love others.

It wasn't that I prayed for God to toughen up the boys, but instead, I asked Him to create in me the man the boys needed. The important point here is to understand that it didn't just happen. The breaking point for those failing blended families usually centers on or involves the children. Here are some tips to do in addition to your prayer life:

- Be Realistic—They're kids who have their own parent(s) and just because their parent loves you doesn't mean they'll love you right away.
- Accept Loss—Maybe you lost a marriage too, and

are protective of your own child. Don't forget that your spouse's kids have also suffered greatly through their own family's failure.

- United Front— You and your spouse must be united. Kids are like running water—they will find the least resistant path, or create one.
- Stay Informed—Your spouse's kids aren't just there to be tolerated. They are unique individuals. Get to know and understand what's going on in their life.
- New Traditions—We all cling to old family customs, but create your own family's memories by starting new traditions.
- No Competition—Your spouse's kids are your responsibility—not your competition.
- Find Support—Don't bail at the first signs of challenge. If it takes family counseling, do it. It's worth the effort.
- Pray for Them—In their presence and in your time, pray for the children in your blended family.
- Pray for Change—Ask God to change you. Pray to have the heart of Jesus when it comes to your blended family.
- Do Right—Like I was told years ago, "Do right by God" before you try doing right by anyone or thing on this earth. God will take care of the rest.

I'll confess. As I wrote this section, I had to stop the "man" slant and write it neutral. This applies across the board. These are universal truths rooted in God's Word.

Truths in Blending

We have a houseful.

To be honest, summer is probably our favorite time of year. We love having all the kids under one roof for an extended period of time.

It's always a bummer when school starts back up, and along with it, the routine of early mornings, after-school band practice, ballet, karate, gymnastics, and wherever else Leah and I find ourselves taxiing the kids. But summer means long, lazy days filled with family time, swimming, BBQing, and fun outings.

I have to admit we're very blessed in the blended family department. We've had a few rough patches over the years, but for the most part, our lives and those of all the kids have melded seamlessly. But...there have been rough patches.

We're talking seven kids, five of which are under eighteen and still live with us, plus the dynamics of Leah and me marrying and creating a new family unit that includes them. Then you have the extended family we created by combining our lives—new grandparents, aunts, uncles, and cousins.

On top of that, the kids have other parents who either remarried or decided to live with someone. Then you add existing children and new children those couples have had together. And then their new grandparents, aunts, uncles, and cousins on that side of the family.

It's no wonder that kids can have a rough transition after their parents divorce. It throws their entire lives into upheaval and introduces a whole lot of new people at one time. We don't use the word *step* in our family, but it's important to remember that a stepparent is a grief trigger in the flesh. They're a constant reminder that their biological parent is no longer part of the constant picture.

You can imagine the confusion, bitterness, or anger from a child if they're not dealing with a "step" parent situation at all, but live-in boyfriends/girlfriends that could revolve in and out of their lives. Kids have no control over their parents' choices. What they want and need are boundaries and stability.

If you're a blended family, please don't get discouraged if your children (or you and your spouse) are having a difficult time adjusting. Like all great things, it takes time, care, and attention.

No, Christian brothers, I do not have that life yet. But I do one thing. I forget everything that is behind me and look forward to that which is ahead of me. My eyes are on the crown. I want to win the race and get the crown of God's call from heaven through Christ Jesus.
Philippians 3:13–14

From the very beginning, I thought Leah and I had it made. I'd spent my career commanding people while accomplishing dangerous and risky missions. How hard could that household of kids be anyway? As we've shared before, family needs engaged parents, not an in-charge chief. What helped us are these seven truths that we developed. Some were stumbled upon by trial and error, and others were intentionally developed to help us stay on track.

1. Priorities

It's going to be really important to set your priorities in front of your children from the beginning. God has to come first. Your marriage has to come second. Your kids come third. Parenting is a temporary assignment. Marriage was designed to last forever.

Children are great at seeing our weak points. If they see chinks in the armor of your marriage they're going to play you against each other. It's important for them to know that the two of you stand together in all things.

It's really easy to get into the habit of putting the kids first. Leah and I were going through old pictures in the garage the other day and we each came across pictures of our kids right after our respective divorces. You can see the sadness and devastation in their eyes, and they're not easy pictures to look at.

When you see that look in their eyes you want to give them whatever you can to make it go away. And it's a completely different dynamic when a new parent comes into the mix. I can tell you from experience this was one of the most challenging things for us, but we also knew it was a necessity. We understood that the kids would adjust quicker with more stability if they knew without a doubt that she and I were rock solid.

2. Disappointments

There are going to be some. Marriage is a big deal. But maybe your kids don't think so. Or maybe your family doesn't think so. Maybe the ideal picture of The Brady Bunch running through your head isn't what reality is like when you get home from your honeymoon. This is the second or third time around after all, right?

Second marriages can succeed by God's grace, work, and commitment to each other. It's much harder, but we serve an awesome God who loves us, no matter what we've done in the past, and who forgives us, as long as we're humble enough to confess and ask for that forgiveness.

We found it helpful to be honest with the children about unmet expectations. It's not uncommon for one or more of them to feel cheated with your attention focused on your new marriage. Maybe it's summer camp that's out of the budget this year, or having to share a room with a sibling. Putting in the work now is the time to make sure that everyone has equity in working through their feelings and expectations. Giving them stability and space to get used to new family dynamics is important.

And as a side note…

When talking about putting the work in at the beginning of your marriage, it's also essential to make sure you and your spouse have alone time at regular intervals so you can connect. But there's only so much alone time you can finagle. That's just parenting life, and it goes with the territory. You'll be empty nesters soon enough.

3. Don't Compare

Don't compare your new marriage, family, life, etc. to the one you had before. It's new territory. It's not a first marriage / first family situation. Don't treat it like one. And don't let your family do it. How many times in your marriage have you heard a family member say, "Well, when he was married to (fill in the blank)…"?

You've both got a past, and it's important you're honest and up front about it. And that you're receptive if your spouse needs to talk about it whenever triggers or issues come up. This goes whether you're a widow/widower or have been divorced. Issues are going to come up. But communication is the key. Not comparison.

4. The Other Parent

Loyalty and Loss are important topics to be sensitive to when it comes to the reality that the kids are loyal to their biological parent, and that they will grieve the loss of access to that parent in their daily life.

Don't talk about the other parent in front of your kids. Loyalties run deep with children to their biological parent. It doesn't matter what the other parent did in the past…if they walked out, if they were unfaithful, if they were a deadbeat…whatever their issues. Your child deserves to not have to worry about grown-up issues. That other person is still their parent, and your children love them, even if you don't.

And another thing to remember…there are probably going to be issues come up with the other parent, and you and your spouse are going to have to discuss it. Don't do it in front of the kids.

5. The Ex

Speaking of the other parent…this can sometimes be more challenging than blending your family. If you have a great relationship with your ex and schedules and lives work smoothly, cherish it. Sometimes it takes years to reach this point. That's cool. Everyone is feeling their way in new territory.

The reality is, you and your spouse each have an ex to deal with. And chances are probably high that at least one of them uses up a lot of your time and energy with drama.

Here's the deal with exes—yes, that other person is the child's parent. But, your spouse and your family that you're blending together are your priority. You've got to have boundaries. Drama from the past and drama from whatever is going on in the ex's life has nothing to do with you or your family. And if they're in a relationship too, it's even less your drama.

There are situations where you'll have an ex text you problems with their new relationship, problems with their own blended family, problems with their finances, problems with work, or problems with wanting more child support. Don't let this become an acceptable practice.

Other than co-parenting a child, this is no longer your life, and anything that doesn't have to do with the child you share together is just them gossiping to you, and potentially "sowing discord" within your new marriage and family.

There are six things that the Lord hates, seven that are an abomination to him: haughty eyes, a lying tongue, and hands that shed innocent blood, a heart that devises wicked plans, feet that make haste to run to evil, a false witness who breathes out lies, and one who sows discord among brothers.
Proverbs 6:16–19

If the ex is having these kinds of issues, they should be confiding in their new spouse or partner, and you need to put down boundaries so they know it's not acceptable behavior.

Let us stress how important boundaries are. You might not think they're that important, especially if you've been putting up with certain behaviors while you were single. But boundaries are going to be essential to your spouse. Boundaries give reassurance. They also create intimacy.

When you don't have boundaries, the ex can easily wreak havoc. It makes your spouse worry and wonder why you're afraid to take a stand for your marriage, and whether the past is really in the past. Unfortunately, there are exes out there that will do everything they can to find cracks in your new marriage and sabotage it. Lay out the boundaries early on so this doesn't happen. Stand together. Stand firm. You'd be surprised how many emails Leah gets from women whose husbands' ex-wives are destroying their marriage.

If you're the spouse with the difficult ex, make sure you're including your new spouse in on everything that's going on. Keeping secrets when dealing with a former relationship is just going to bring up worry, doubt, and trust issues. Being up front from the beginning can eliminate these problems.

If you're the spouse who is watching your husband/wife deal with a difficult ex, be patient and remember the two of you are a team. It's sometimes difficult to imagine that your husband/wife could've picked both you and the ex from the same planet, especially if the ex is really difficult or drama-prone.

It's very easy to let satan wedge his way in by using that ex to cause problems in your marriage. Remember, satan hates marriage. He'll do whatever he can to destroy it. The two of you have to do what's best for your marriage and your family. The ex is an adult. They can handle their own problems, choices, and drama without dragging you down the rabbit hole.

Outside of having a set schedule, the only way that you can allow their drama to enter your life is if you let them. This is why it's extremely important to have legal custody decrees and everything in writing. Hot button topics such as more child support are easily dictated by each state with a formula based on income. Even if you get along great with an ex, I still recommend having set terms in writing and filed with the court. There could be a day when the ex isn't so friendly and it's a lot harder to negotiate terms at that point. Protect yourself and your family.

6. Schedules Get Crazy!

This we know from experience. When Leah and I got married she had four kids and I had three. Now we have seven. Five of which live under our roof because they're still young. There are days when we are crazy outnumbered. We really have to communicate and have good calendars to make sure everyone gets everywhere they're supposed to be. It's challenging and insane. But we have fun doing it, and I think we've got it down to a pretty good science. At least until school starts again and we have to remember what we were doing.

And look, I'll be honest, if we can make schedules work, anyone can make schedules work. Leah and I work an insane amount of hours a week (usually in the middle of the night while the kids are sleeping), and we travel around one hundred days of the year (for work). We schedule all of it around the kids' custody schedules, though sometimes we do have to make adjustments to the schedule with the other parents. But it works. Because we put in the time to make it work. You can do it! We promise!

We took our very first trip this year without laptops for an actual vacation and we both survived!

7. You Will Love Your Spouse's Children

It's hard to imagine loving any children like you love your own. But it will happen. If you're putting your priorities in the right order (God, marriage, children), it will happen. You'll worry about their futures, you'll hug them when they're hurt or just need a snuggle, you'll hold them to the same expectations as your biological children, and you'll also discipline them the same way. It might not happen overnight, but it will happen.

Behold, children are a heritage from the Lord, the fruit of the womb a reward. Like arrows in the hand of a warrior are the children of one's youth. Blessed is the man who fills his quiver with them! He shall not be put to shame when he speaks with his enemies in the gate.
Psalm 127:3–5

We all make mistakes as parents. But if Christ is the center of your marriage, and you and your spouse make your marriage a priority, your children are going to benefit. Even with divorce in your past, it's possible to start building a godly legacy by the blending of your families.

Parents: Past and Present

I was only two years on the job prior to my first promotion, but an opportunity for a motivated young officer to make a difference presented itself and I was there to accept it. In August 1992, I was promoted as the commander over a multi-jurisdictional drug and violent crimes task force. From then, until my retirement as chief of police in August 2015, I held leadership positions at a large nationally accredited agency. I've served as a division commander over a detective bureau, special ops section, and uniform patrol division.

In addition to my twelve years in an undercover narcotics unit, and sixteen years on SWAT, I finished my career with the last five as the chief of police. I've been in the thick of things for a long time. One of the most important lessons I've learned about leading people is knowing how to serve them. Aptly enough called "Servant Leadership."

I've had many rookies over the years ask when they would get promoted. It was sometimes distressing as not every situation was about an eagerness to lead, but the assumed status they selfishly sought over their peers. My response was pretty typical: "Once you've learned to serve." Of course, that wasn't the answer they wanted.

I have set you an example that you should do as I have done for you.
Very truly I tell you, no servant is greater than his master, nor is a
messenger greater than the one who sent him. Now that you know these
things, you will be blessed if you do them.
John 13:15–17

The lessons I learned during those years of leading also apply to the most important leadership role you will ever fulfill. Being a parent to your biological child can be challenging. Being a parent in a blended family can be downright tough.

Your child has known you and your ways since conception. Blended kids have no base of reference other than you're the new adult in their parent's life who also isn't their other biological parent. Talk about a tough crowd!

Believe it or not, it's usually the adult who bails on the blended family by giving up on their spouse's child, rather than the other way around. What most stepparents admit is feeling like they have to compete with the kids for the affection of their new spouse. Guess what? When you marry their parent, the kids are your responsibility, not your competition.

These are five truths I've crafted during my career. They've served me well having moved up the ranks from a rookie patrolman to a city's top cop. I also use them daily as the chief in my own blended household.

1. Never lie to them—This should seem simple, but it's not. Don't lie even about the smallest of things.
2. Never speak harshly to them—Spirit-crushing words rarely heal and are seldom forgotten.
3. Always lead from the front—There's a huge difference in "Go" versus "Let's Go."
4. Consistent in discipline—No one responds well to wavering behavior that teeters on varying ends of the spectrum.
5. Trust but confirm—You're still in a position of authority and must ensure that they are following the rules.

Focus on finding or creating small scenarios where you can teach the child or children something you know or enjoy. Have patience, and use the moments to build common ground, not to punish them for unfamiliarity.

While it may be easy to boss kids around, practice holding yourself to a higher standard of mentoring. They don't need a job site foreman, they need a decent adult who won't let them down. And who knows, you might end up enjoying them after all.

I'll share with you a little bit more about my experiences with parenting. The first time I was married, we had a son. I was so in love with him and still am, but I wasn't mentored to be a dad. Out of desperation, I did what I thought I should do, or maybe even what I saw dads on TV do.

The end result was that I thought the best way to be a dad and a husband was to throw myself into work. I was providing for my family. That's what husbands and dads did, right? While that made me a very productive drug agent, it did nothing on the home front. Not surprisingly, we were divorced by the time my son was four years old.

Parents, past and present, aren't that different. Because the old adage, an apple doesn't fall far from the tree, is true. I did what my dad did, and he did what his dad did. I only pray that once my son has his own family, that he'll break the generational cycle of workaholic, disengaged fathers.

Before we get much further, no matter what the relationship with your father looked like, it is important that we respect God's command to honor our father (and mother). Even if he bolted on you as a kid, it's still not our place to judge him.

Honor your father and your mother, so your life may be long in the land the Lord your God gives you.
Exodus 20:12

Matthew 7:1–3 is one of our favorite instructions. Judge not, less ye be judged. You know that everything we have criticized and placed the condemnation of judgment upon our dads is what we're most likely to become. I resented my dad's emotional distance, and swore that my kids would never once go without knowing that I loved them.

I believe because of my judgments, my sons knew I loved them in word, but not in action. My love for police work trumped the quality time I should've spent with them.

Judge not, that ye be not judged. For with what judgment ye judge, ye shall be judged: and with what measure ye mete, it shall be measured unto you. And why beholdest thou the mote that is in thy brother's eye, but considerest not the beam that is in thine own eye?
Matthew 7:1–3

Everything we do as parents sets a generational chain reaction in motion. Kids of divorce usually become divorced adults. Similar to alcoholics parenting alcoholics, and abusers who abuse. We only know what we know. As I confessed, while my heart deeply desired a loving commitment to my son, all I knew was to show my "fatherhood" by working to provide.

The good news is, we have the power to break the chains of iniquity that have been passed on to us, not just from our parents or grandparents, but from the very first couple in existence. Once we shatter those generational curses, we pave the way for future generations to know God's love and blessing.

Keeping mercy for thousands, forgiving iniquity and transgression and sin, and that will by no means clear the guilty; visiting the iniquity of the fathers upon the children, and upon the children's children, unto the third and to the fourth generation.
Exodus 34:7

If you had a wonderful relationship with your parents and their model served as the model you now use in a happy, Christ-centered marriage, then hallelujah. If that's what you're doing and it works, keep on doing it.

But if you're like Leah and me, who have traveled the long route to get to our happy place, it's okay. You also have the spiritual authority to set your path, and the path for your children. Even kids of divorce rebound when their parent(s) shows a remarriage example of a loving, covenant marriage. Whether your folks were Ozzie and Harriet or Ozzie and Sharon, you now set the course from this moment forward. Chart that course wisely.

Mixing Faith and Family

Just when you think you've got it figured out, here comes a doozie. This is even more challenging than which arm to put that new blue line tattoo on. Combining different faiths often makes it impossible. Unless God is in the mix of course! If you haven't yet, now is the perfect time to have this discussion with your spouse, along with the ton of other challenges involved with blending families.

The positive side is that there are generally three options that form the basis of this discussion. One or both of you are:

1. Very God centered.
2. Somewhat God centered.
3. Not God centered.

Don't take this as any shade of judgment, but it's an important part of blended families. The truth is, it's very rare that both partners are at the same place in their spiritual walk at the same time. Seriously, this is the perfect time to really open up.

Leah and I had different paths toward faith. It was each other's understanding and support that gave us the time and space to understand where each other was in our walk with Christ. It was one of the very few things we didn't fight about because it was one of the first things we discussed.

Conversations about faith can get intense, so that's why it's important that ground rules are set before the first defensive response starts to fly. It's not about comparing who is more religious or a better person. That wouldn't be very Christian now would it? The most common issue we see is that there are different religions involved, and that usually brings various traditions and expectations.

In a realistic way, talk about how tied you each are to your faith. How does each one's faith affect your daily lives in a tangible way? For example, does your religion require certain diets, mandatory prayer throughout the day, numerous holy days, abstinence from certain clothes, activities, birth control, or sexual practices to name a few?

Next, identify areas of flexibility—Can Jewish kids partake in Christmas / will a nonbeliever's kids partake in Easter? Your level of commitment to your faith will usually equal your ability to be flexible for the family's sake. If there is no room for flexibility, is it because of being close-minded or that one of you is so devoutly faithful that you just won't bend? We're not suggesting either of you sacrifice your faith, but understand the difference between rituals, traditions, and practicing true faith.

This section can get really sensitive, but it's also important to discuss. Another high-risk situation is if one of you is a believer and the other one is not. In the bible, Paul talked about being unequally yoked with a nonbeliever. The biblical preference is to avoid conjoining, but if patrol officers and narcotics agents can work together, then there's hope for everyone.

Do not be unequally yoked with unbelievers. For what partnership has righteousness with lawlessness? Or what fellowship has light with darkness?
2 Corinthians 6:14

So like we said, there is still hope because God provides for the differences.

To the rest I say (I, not the Lord) that if any brother has a wife who is an unbeliever, and she consents to live with him, he should not divorce her. If any woman has a husband who is an unbeliever, and he consents to live with her, she should not divorce him. For the unbelieving husband is made holy because of his wife, and the unbelieving wife is made holy because of her husband. Otherwise your children would be unclean, but as it is, they are holy.
1 Corinthians 7:12–14

Let's simplify this with a few well-placed bullet points:

- Be open to discussing not only what you want, but why faith-based practices are important. Do you have to attend Easter sunrise service because it has deep spiritual value, because it's what you did as a child, or because you want to go early and have the rest of the day free?
- In order for both spouses to have an honest talk, each must understand what faith means to them so they can explain it to each other. Sometimes couples realize faith or religion doesn't have that big of an impact in their lives. Should your marriage or kids suffer because one spouse demands doing something without having an attachment to it?
- Faith and depth of spirituality may shift through time. Make sure it is a regular conversation.
- Unless there is some unique court order, most kids practice or don't practice the faith of the parent who has custody.
- Explain to kids that the other parent does things different or not at all, but that doesn't make one parent right or wrong.
- Neither parent should force faith or practices upon children, and must respect the other parent's beliefs. Even the atheist should not be demonized for not believing in God.
- Parents must prevent in-laws from meddling—Catholic baptisms by grandparents of non-Catholic children have caused so many serious problems, and led to a few arrests for kidnapping and assault (no kidding).
- Parents must agree before having children participate in religious ritualistic acts or "certifications"—taking communion for example, ritualistic cuttings, or water baptism.

Here are a few basic tips to avoid the "religious" rub, and ensure that you approach faith in a faithful manner.

1. Have a plan.
2. Agree on how to observe traditions associated with each faith.

3. Share your point of view without being defensive or making unkind remarks about the other's faith, or absence of one.
4. Faith is definitely a "hot button," but this decision is really no different from any other decision you must make when combining families.
5. In custodial matters, accept that whoever has the kid, has the custom.
6. In a blended family, agree to compromise and always refer back to #1.

The biblical standard is that God must be placed as the head of your marriage. Your spouse comes next, and kids are third in the faith hierarchy. We know that many parents in a blended family scenario place the kids as priority, but that is a mistake and usually leads to divorce.

Your kids need to see the adults focusing on God, and then each other. They will not be loved any less or feel left out. Kids from divorce often grow up to divorce. But if they have a solid blended family example done right, it reduces their risk of divorcing as an adult.

This is your insurance:

Train up a child in the way he should go,
And when he is old he will not depart from it.
Proverbs 22:6

9

SEX

What Does God Say?

It's funny, because Leah's mother still whispers when she says the word *sex*. It's not like she throws it around all day, but typical of her depression-era generation, that word still holds a naughty connotation that's best left behind closed doors. The irony is, when we talk with our kids, we also find ourselves either wanting to whisper the word, or tiptoe around the topic to ease the tension by making light of it.

Let's face it, sex isn't the easiest thing to talk about unless it's among the guys in the squad room, or the gals while chatting over a glass of wine. Sex has found itself in a peculiar situation. Although God created it to be enjoyed between a husband and wife, the world has perverted it to the point where we act like the devil holds the deed to it.

Maybe it's the stigma that God created sex that makes it seem stoic, or in order to really enjoy it, we must keep it a secret. Too often we get caught up on the downside of thinking it can't be fun because God is serious business. Guess what? God created humor too.

God designed us to experience the pleasure of sex. Think about that for a few seconds. There is no other reason for a clitoris other than for pleasure. I know the world has forced us to believe the lie that married sex is boring. Satan's goal is to pervert all other avenues of the flesh. But the truth is, God is still very much in charge, and you can have the best sex of your life—with your spouse.

So what does God have to say about sex? I know most people begin to roll their eyes or emotionally check out when the topic is mentioned. But it's really very interesting, and it also gets very sensual.

Let him kiss me with the kisses of his mouth. For your love is better than wine.
– Song of Songs 1:2

One thing the bible is not when it comes to sex, is a list of thou shalt nots. Nowhere in God's Word will you find a list of instructions for the way married people must engage in procreation. Did you know that we are one of the rare species that have the ability to mate while looking at each other face to face?

Go ahead. We'll give you a few moments to think back through the National Geographic episodes you've seen, or a few random pet hookups you might've witnessed while out jogging. Okay, now that you're back, isn't that interesting?

Why did God design it that way?

Because copulation between animals for the purpose of procreation is the mechanical process of replicating their species. Humans, on the other hand, were created in God's image and meant for relationships. One of the strongest bonding agents for a relationship is sex and the physiological effects of engaging in it.

The eyes are truly the windows to the soul. What better way to relate one-to-one than through soul-deep stares while reaffirming your marriage covenant through sex?

Marriage is not a civil contract It's a bible-based covenant between you, your spouse, and God. Covenants are not entered into to be broken, and they also require a seal. Sex is the covenant seal of marriage. Or, as Leah likes to call it, the "sticky glue" that keeps us together. Yeah, I know, she's a handful, but she's right.

Now that we've agreed there is much more to married sex than the missionary position with the lights off, let's take a look at key scriptures regarding sex. While God created it to be pleasing to the husband and wife, there must be safeguards in place to protect anything of value. Scripture provides for those protective boundaries.

Breaking those boundaries has consequences. The offense is sin, and the consequence is separation from God. What are the tangible consequences of sex beyond the marriage boundary? Divorce, depression, disease, abortion, and suicide to roll off a few of the big ones. Then there's children born out of wedlock; child support; alimony; counseling; attorneys; loss of respect, career, and social status once friends begin taking sides.

Not to be a downer, but any of these, and so many more, terrible scenarios are possible just because of what? A flirt, a smile, boredom, a quid pro quo to get out of a citation, or a proposition while working an off-duty detail at the club. Were the clandestine moments of an adulterous affair worth the lifetime of consequences for breaking the holy vow sworn before your wife and before God?

Let's look at a key scripture, and you tell me what you think God is trying to tell us. The sanctity of marriage is affirmed in Hebrews with a very straightforward and powerful word about sex and sin.

Marriage is to be honored by all, and husbands and wives must be faithful to each other. God will judge those who are immoral and those who commit adultery.
Hebrews 13:4

I'm not sure about you, but as far as marital sex advice goes, it doesn't get much better or more simple than that. The words that jump out at me are Honor—Faithful—Judge. In law enforcement these words are key descriptors of what job we do, and how we feel about doing the job. If we're willing to lay our life down for strangers based on these key words, then why can't we lay down our temptations for sexual sin?

Sexual sin didn't start in the 1960s era of free love. Mankind has struggled with it from the very beginning of time. Sex is a frequent topic in both the Old and New Testaments. God knows our need for sex and also our weaknesses when sex is involved. He warns us about being caught up in this world and what our three most destructive threats are.

- Lust of the eye.
- Lust of the flesh.
- Prideful spirit.

For everything in the world—the lust of the flesh, the lust of the eyes, and the pride of life—comes not from the Father but from the world.
1 John 2:16

Affairs don't start in the bedroom. They start with a glance, and a returned look. A longing gaze at their body and an acknowledgement that it's pleasing to see and a stimulation to the fantasy of thought. Affairs come to fruition because the married offender is conceited with a prideful spirit into thinking it's okay this one time, their spouse will never find out, or God will forgive them.

Is living the shady life that important for filling a void in your spirit? If so, there's much more going down than an overactive sex drive. There is no peace in darkness, but there is pleasure in the light of purity and a vibrant, healthy sex life with your spouse.

"Yeah, but it's hard with all that temptation."

It's only hard if you create the circumstances that allow it to become a temptation. The best way to handle it is found in where else? God's Word.

Flee from sexual immorality. All other sins a person commits are outside the body, but whoever sins sexually, sins against their own body.
1 Corinthians 6:18

Connected and committed is the way God intended you to share your life, and also your marriage bed. It's so important to understand that Genesis 2:24 is the foundational rock upon which marriage is based.

The process of building your marriage into a bulletproof team does not allow for including others into your sex life. Whether it's the fantasy of another person, the physical presence of another person, or pornography, it violates the core of Genesis. It says the two shall become one. Nowhere in there does it talk about a threesome. It also goes the same for porn. Mental and emotional adultery is just as destructive as physical. When you go outside of the attraction your spouse brings, it's an offense to the gift that God created just for you.

But since sexual immorality is occurring, each man should have sexual relations with his own wife, and each woman with her own husband.
1 Corinthians 7:2

When You're Not in the Mood

Leah and I were at a marriage conference, and the pastor, who we adore, was talking about the joy of sex. Then he began to touch on the truths of sex, and that it's unrealistic to expect both people to be in the mood at the exact same time. He said that he and his wife understood the importance of intimate time together, so when he wanted sex, he'd tell her, "Honey, I want sex."

I tapped Leah on the arm and said, "Honey, I want sex."

She rolled her eyes and patted me on the thigh. So much for figuring out how women work. Maybe that's how it works for an old country pastor, but for most of us, there are other paths to be explored. But the truth is, sex, kids, and cash are the top three fight starters for married couples, so let's get to the bottom of it.

LEO marriages have the reality of shift work, overtime, and off-duty details contributing to physical and emotional fatigue. The chances of a twelve-hour shifter being on the same amorous cycle as their nine-to-five spouse is rare. This is where conflict starts. But we're going to look at ways to preempt the pitfalls.

And just in case what worked for that pastor, also works for you, then disregard what we're about to share and head into the bedroom for some of that good old-fashioned country lovin'.

But seriously, sex is a big deal. It's God's covenant seal for marriage. Even in a hyper-secularized world, some states do not consider marriage legal until it has been consummated. Where did that standard come from? God's Word in Genesis 2:24 of course. The two shall become one. If you find yourself going days, weeks, or even... gasp...months, and if you've suffered without sex because one or both of you aren't in the mood, then this lesson is for you.

Remember those days of lying in bed all weekend, making love and only rolling out of each other's arms when the dog scratched on the door to go outside? What happens to those marathon honeymoon sex sessions? How do we go from "baby love me one more time" to "love is a battlefield"?

Sex is so important that in the very first book of the bible, God's first instruction to man and woman was to be fruitful and increase in number. I think that's pretty self-explanatory, don't you? Now, if the shift sergeant told you to hit the streets and fill the jail with warrant arrests, there'd be no stopping you, but are you pursuing marital passion with the same vigor as chasing felons?

So God created mankind in his own image, in the image of God he created them; male and female he created them.
God blessed them and said to them, "Be fruitful and increase in number; fill the earth and subdue it. Rule over the fish in the sea and the birds in the sky and over every living creature that moves on the ground."
Genesis 1:27–28

The problem post-honeymoon isn't as much that neither wants sex, but is that communication gets crossed when one wants it and the other doesn't. This isn't the time to panic or begin making accusations against each other.

We've mentioned that love is a choice, and not an emotion. While that reality may take some of the allure out of *amore*, it should serve as a reassurance to both of you that neither have to worry about falling out of love. You choose to love or not to love; there is no falling where your relationship is concerned. Well, except for falling into bed.

Anger, rejection, and abandonment are often the net results when one partner feels that their sexual needs are not being met. While sex is one of the top categories couples divorce over, it's rarely ever a topic of discussion. It's mired in so much complexity, because as a society we still fail in having open, mature conversations about sex.

It wasn't uncommon for me to come home after duty and go from one extreme to the other. If the day was especially stressful, allowing Leah to enter my space was the last thing on my mind. I'd reject her without considering that she had no clue what had gone on during my day. But, like most of us cops, the stress isn't something we want to talk about. So our spouse is shut down and shut out.

Once Leah's heart was hurt by my rejection, her depth of pain was felt deeper because she had an expectation of sharing intimacy with me in our marriage bed. Because her expectation was high (rightly so), and my cold rejection was so swift, she was left with a deficit that was difficult to talk about. After all, I'd just shut her down for intimacy. How in the world would that conversation have turned out for you?

On the other side of the pendulum is when I'd knock off of duty and head home amped up over a big day or a closed case. There wasn't much talking then either as I expected her to be there for the ravishing. That mostly works in the movies, but not when your spouse has had their own stressful day and isn't in the mood.

Either way it started, it almost always ended with the anger of rejection by one and the wounds of disrespect by the other. Let's not beat around the bush, it's hard to stop and say, "I wanted sex, but you hurt my feelings." Honestly, I couldn't imagine anyone saying it that way, but the point is, we'd rather allow the separation of unreliable emotions to dominate our relationship.

Sex in marriage is too important to not talk about. We talk about it all the time before we're married, so why not when it really matters? It's an old truth that we spend all of our time trying to get each other into bed before marriage, and the devil makes sure we stay out of it after we're married.

Desire discrepancy is a fancy way of saying one of you is not in the mood. It happens more often than most couples would think. Actually, over 80 percent of married couples who participated in a sex study reported struggling with one or the other not being in the mood for sex over the month prior to the interview. The same study also reported that desire discrepancy occurred five out of seven days per week throughout the course of the one-month testing period.

It happens because we're human, and life gets in the way. So now that we know there's a really cool research term (desire discrepancy) for not being in the mood, we can move forward to handle it like a rock solid, Blue Marriage couple should.

A result from the same study showed that spouses who were not in the mood, yet still had sex with their spouse, have stronger tendencies to place the needs of their loved one above those of themselves without an expectation of reciprocation. This isn't tit for tat, it's about doing as God's Word commands.

Do not deprive one another, except perhaps by agreement for a limited time, that you may devote yourselves to prayer; but then come together again, so that Satan may not tempt you because of your lack of self-control.
1 Corinthians 7:5

And to wrap up this train of thought, the spouse who wasn't in the mood, yet had sex just to please their spouse, ended up reaping benefits from the act of having physical intimacy. The physiological effects of chemical responses in the body benefit both spouses regardless of their emotional motives. So not to beat up on emotions, but simply relying on them isn't a good practice or principle for building marital muscle.

And while Leah and I are sure this goes without saying, coercing or forcing your spouse into having sex when they're not up to it does not have the same benefit. So despite one's desire to give when giving isn't an option, the taker must respect that there are times when receiving does the opposite for bonding the relationship.

Sex is the ultimate way of serving our spouse, and only your spouse can meet that need. Women typically tend to have a lesser sex drive than men, and that's perfectly okay. That's how God made us. But sex is one of the most important priorities of your marriage. I don't care if you have to schedule a day and time on the calendar to come together each week, it's worth it. Do you have periods of time where you're short tempered with each other and fighting a lot? When was the last time you had sex? The longer you go without it, the wider the chasm for having intimacy in your marriage.

We know it's hard to do, but instead of waiting to talk until one of you gets angry or rejected, why not do it now. Or right after reading this section, or having sex! Here are a few ideas for moving forward when one of you is lagging behind.

Forge Ahead

Marriage is about sacrifice. We give and take because the in-betweens are where the real, deep connections are created in a relationship.

Anticipation

If you're not a fan of spontaneity, then charge up your sexual engine by thinking about having sex with your spouse as you go through the day. Especially for wives, the mind is a big part of sexual preps, so set your mind ablaze, and your body will follow.

Examination

Take time to reflect about why it is that you're not in the mood. Just proclaiming or avoiding it doesn't solve anything. Identify the cause(s) and if one of the reasons is your spouse, then have that mature conversation.

Stoke the Fire

You're both different. Now where have you heard that before? God truly does have a sense of humor. Appeal to each other's needs. This is something ladies need to focus on. I can say that because my wife is standing right here telling me to say that. Women tend to get busy with kids, schedules, work, dinner, and any of the other hundreds of tasks they make look so effortless. But your spouse is your priority. Meet each other's needs. Send sexy texts to each other, or set aside time after the kids go to bed instead of zoning in front of the TV. Get up twenty minutes early, or share a shower.

Negotiations

Instead of a flat rejection of no, how about offering alternatives such as specifying another time if they're willing to be patient. Maybe it's after a nap so the headache subsides, or once the kids are asleep so there's no distraction. Anything but a terse no. Rejection hurts. Truth without love is just mean.

The big takeaway from all of this is to talk before one is driven by desire and the other is just driven away. Make sure you both understand that the body's own cycle of physical need may run along different tracks on occasion. That's okay, because you're both heading in the same direction together.

What Is Taboo?

I was sitting in my chief's office about two weeks before Leah and I were set to be married. In addition to reviewing police reports, talking to the media, the mayor and other executive duties, I had officers regularly stop in. Some talked about their pride in doing the job, others complained about doing the job, but most came in at the very end of their rope.

It seems cops are masters at helping everyone else get their lives straight, but horrible at figuring out their own. I'd listen to pleas for promotion and overtime because they couldn't afford child support, or that they were applying to another agency for pennies more an hour because they were going through a divorce, and needed the extra cash to pay for their upcoming wedding, and, well, I could go on, but we all live this life every day.

The point is, on that certain day, an officer who I mentored asked if I was ever getting married. I'd been single for almost twenty years, and to anyone who didn't really know me, it looked like bachelorhood was my destiny. Because I trusted him, I confided that I was indeed getting married, and very soon. He was shocked.

The single, young guy said, "You're going to be so bored having sex with the same woman for the rest of your life."

While I don't think he'd actually thought about it before saying it, his gut response highlighted the typical thought about married sex. Whoever started the old myth that married couples can only do the missionary position really needs an ASP baton to the shin.

Think back to Adam and Eve. They were the perfect couple. He didn't have a grumpy desk sergeant to deal with and she didn't have to worry about her friends running them down on Facebook because the hubs arrested someone's tenth cousin for his fifth DUI. They were free, and they were naked. Not just from clothing, but in their relationship to each other.

They worked hard managing the garden of Eden, and they hung out with each other with no secrets, no shame, and no sin. They didn't even have mama baby daddy issues. It was truly paradise. On top of that, God Himself hung out with them in the cool of the day to walk and talk.

Can you imagine the most intimate level of relationship and transparency as you and your wife talk with God? The point we're making is that Adam and Eve were open books before God. Sin had not entered the garden to create the separation between them and God. They were as close as possible, and in the midst of that closeness, Adam and Eve were instructed to be fruitful and multiply.

I know we're all aware of what being fruitful and multiplying means, and to do that also requires something we don't give God the credit for creating—sex.

Not to belabor that point, but if we're going to talk about sex, and whether or not anything is taboo in the course of intercourse, then we need to have a clear understanding that sex isn't some by-product of the naughty things we do in the dark. Making love is as natural as breathing. It's healthy for you, and is good for your health. It's not only created by God, but it's encouraged by Him as well.

But like everything valuable, there are boundaries surrounding sex. The caveat is that sex was created for marriage, not casual hookups and booty calls. This is where the dark side distorts the reality of a really good thing.

To be clear, we're talking about sex between a man and woman who are married to each other. In this context, the simple answer about what is taboo in sex might surprise you. The answer is…nothing. There is nothing taboo in sex between a husband and wife. Okay, before you start stammering about, "Yeah, but," please put every negative thing you've heard, been told, or thought out of your mind. As long as you both consent, and you're not bringing in a third party, you're good to go.

We work in a world where facts mean guilt or no guilt, so we want to share just the facts as they're presented in God's Word. Nowhere in the bible will you find a do and don't list for sex between husband and wife. The only stipulation is that both spouses consent to whatever act is exercised.

Of course, this doesn't mean you have to sign off on an agreement before trying something tricky, but part of sharing the blessing of God's gift to the married couple is that you honor each other as you would honor God. If it's mutually pleasing to each of you, then God is pleased. Somehow married people who are struggling have the notion that marital sex is supposed to be boring. That's the reason they are struggling.

We're banking that you've still got questions about this because it almost seems too good to be true. We get the oral sex questions all the time. Again, as long as you both discuss it, agree to it, and enjoy it, then it's yours as a married couple.

Adam and his wife were both naked, and they felt no shame.
Genesis 2:25

Let's put a red satin bow around this with a huge dose of truth. As wonderful as the reality of sexual freedom is between a husband and wife, it's equally horrific when sex is taken outside of that boundary. We keep repeating the phrase "sex between the husband and wife" for a reason. Sex outside of the marriage bed is a huge no-no, with equally serious consequences.

Marriage should be honored by all, and the marriage bed kept pure,
for God will judge the adulterer and all the sexually immoral.
Hebrews 13:4

We know so many cops struggle with sexual sin and pornography. We'd say the number of cops addicted to porn is similar to that of the civilian population. But the incidents of cops shackled in sexual bondage is increased exponentially because of dynamics associated with the job.

It's not that law enforcement causes sexual sin, but by the very nature of its secret society, alpha male chauvinistic environment, and above-the-law ethos, it attracts the preinclined and presents an avenue of access to easy targets.

Like I said earlier, there is nothing off limits to sex within the boundaries of the marriage bed, but there are restrictions. We're also asked about masturbation, sex toys, and pornography. We know masturbation keeps us from giving our whole selves to our spouse, especially if we've satisfied our own needs. But there's nothing to say you can't masturbate during sex with each other. As long as you're pleasing each other.

Everything is permissible, but not everything is beneficial. Everything is permissible—but not everything is constructive. Nobody should seek his own good, but the good of others.
1 Corinthians 10:23–24

Pornography on the other hand, doesn't get off so easy. This is not only a marriage killer, but it destroys your career, your brain, and your life. The devil attacks us in distinctive areas involving lust and pride. It's no different from inviting a third or fourth person into your marriage bed. Do not do that.

The only thing God commands is that you stay monogamous, both physically and mentally. The apostle Paul gave some guidelines to the Corinthian church:

But since sexual immorality is occurring, each man should have sexual relations with his own wife, and each woman with her own husband.
1 Corinthians 7:2

This is especially good advice for cops because it's one of the most sexually promiscuous cultures out there. I'm calling it like it is because of the connection to past personal pain, authoritarian power, and a quest for controlling conquests. When these interpersonal dynamics are mixed with the autonomy of groupthink behind a mystical thin blue line of us versus them, it's a ready recipe for deviant behavior.

Please, a shift wife may seem exciting and easy to get away with, but every time you step outside of the protective boundary of the marriage covenant, you're placing yourself, your spouse, your kids, and your career in jeopardy. This is why it was told to rookies for decades before me, and continues to be told to rookies today, "Your badge will get you sex, but sex will get your badge."

Enjoy the no-limits sexual pleasures with your beloved wife, and gain God's blessing. It'll be the hottest sex you've ever had.

Past Sexual Regrets

"I'm a whore."

Her comment caught me off guard. I never made it a habit of meeting with women alone in my office. Not even female officers. Depending on the situation, I'd either have my female administrative assistant sit in, or another officer.

This was a senior officer who I'd known for years. I also knew her husband on a personal level, and unless it was just she and I, she refused to go through with the meeting she requested.

Before she blurted out that declaration, we sat in silence. As you well know, there is never a right way of predicting what a cop will talk about when they request a private meeting.

Honestly, I laughed a little when she said it because what else could she have been doing but joking. Right? She didn't laugh. She reassured me that she was serious, and I began to glance through the glass window in the door between my admin and me. Like clockwork, she was watching and waiting for a signal to intervene.

Only this time, I saw the darkened expression of this officer, my friend's face, and she was wounded. It was time to stop worrying about being PC, and start acting like her long-time friend.

She didn't cry, as I thought she might, but she detailed that the pain from her past haunted her. She'd been married for several years, but her husband didn't know anything much about her past before they met. She was a cop and single mom when they met, and he loved her. End of story, and no need going backward to a time before he knew her.

Unfortunately, her husband's unknowing didn't resolve her guilt over a promiscuous past. I'd heard stories through the grapevine, but I was always cautious to avoid getting caught up in salacious squad-room talk. It was all too common and fed a daily diet of the police rumor mill.

Her past had started to chip away at the wonderful wife, mother, and cop she'd worked so hard to become. She was allowing her past to define her, and that's right where the devil wants us to be. As long as we're mourning our dark past, we aren't anticipating our glorious future with Christ.

Unless we were born on Monday and married on Tuesday, we all bring baggage to the marriage. Admittedly, some baggage is the size of the Superdome, while others could stash it in a penny pocket.

I was fifty years old when Leah and I married. I'd also been divorced almost twenty years before we'd met. Had I dated? Yes. A lot? Yes. Were there consequences for sexual sin? Of course. Overcoming past sexual experiences requires trust, transparency, and healing. Let's not kid ourselves, promiscuity runs rampant among the first responder community. That goes for men and women.

I believe it's because there is a world of unresolved hurt hidden deep in the souls of the bravest. We carry our pain into a profession riddled with hurting people who hurt other people. No wonder we suffer. Instead of finding safety among the brethren to put pieces back together, we're force-marched into the alpha-male matrix of public service's macho expectations.

But when real healing isn't available because it's frowned upon by the profession, sex is often used to help hide the hurt. Even if it's a one-night stand where manufactured intimacy is generated, sex is still a powerful form of medicating pain. Unfortunately, it leads to regrettable sexual experiences that follow us into our new relationships.

Truth must be told when trust is gained that your partner will receive it with understanding and no judgment. If you or both of you were survivors of rape or abuse, it affects your relationship's ability to grow into deep intimacy. Sharing your story with your spouse can lead to healing.

Even if the sexual regrets resulted from consensual encounters, the creeping sense of conviction begins to conflict with your attempts to conceal a sordid past. Whether it's a one-night stand or a hundred separate conquests, sex comes with a price. The payment is usually demanded through your silent shame.

In police work, we get used to the repetition of handling one case and then moving on to the next. Little thought is given to the last case unless it begins to infringe on our current or future investigations. The victims become no more than names and offense codes entered into our records management system. But in time, we come to understand that the victims are not ghosts, and their stories have made an impression upon our soul.

It's the same thing about sex. Society claims to have liberated sex by freeing it from the marital bedroom and spreading it out in the open. They say married-only sex is repressive and instead, encourage what they've termed "free sex."

Well, guess what? Sex isn't free. There's a cost associated with it, and in the context of sex outside of marriage, the cost is called sin. And God is very clear about the wages of sin:

For the wages of sin is death, but the free gift of God is eternal life in
Christ Jesus our Lord.
Romans 6:23

Death in this context is separation from God, unless you've contracted an STD that will lead to your actual physical death. Otherwise, it's a separation that means living your life in a spiritual death similar to Adam and Eve when they were banished from paradise and daily fellowship with God.

In addition to the spiritual cost of sexual sin, the physical debt is a great expense as well. The reason you carry regrets is because sex is like a glue. Now, if it's sex between you and your spouse, that glue is the covenant seal of marriage, and helps ensure the security of that relationship. Sex outside of marriage is a very different sticky situation.

Sex was purposefully intended to be a powerful force for joining two people together in marriage. We've covered this before when talking about Genesis in chapters one and two. God's first instruction to His creations was to be fruitful and multiply. The next chapter describes Adam and Eve becoming one flesh. Yes, that means they had sex. How important do you think sex is in the grand scheme of God's design?

We feel the regrets because we've bought into the lie that sex is just physical, and if consensual, there are no obligations. This is a giant lie. Every time we "become one" with someone, whether it's your spouse (Genesis 2:24) or with a prostitute (1 Corinthians 6:16), we imprint ourselves physically and spiritually.

Do you not know that he who unites himself with a prostitute is one with her in body? For it is said, "The two will become one flesh."
1 Corinthians 6:16

In addition to God designing sex to bond us as one flesh through physical intimacy, we're also connected through the release of the pleasure chemical, oxytocin. By complete heavenly design, the chemical is naturally released in significant quantities only three times in a woman's life, and only once for men. Oxytocin is released when a woman gives birth and when she breastfeeds. Both of these releases are so that a maternal bond is created with the child.

The third time for the woman and the only time a man releases oxytocin is when both are enjoying sexual arousal and release. Oxytocin is what binds us together. It's a beautiful thing between husband and wife. It's not so beautiful when it occurs between unmarried partners because the bonds remain long after the orgasm has passed.

Like my friend who confessed to sex with between fifteen to twenty-something partners, there's a physical, spiritual, and physiological tie that has bound her to every one of them, whether she knew their name or not. And now her husband is connected to all of those anonymous men as well.

If you're struggling to break through and experience a deep intimacy with your spouse, but you just can't seem to get past something keeping you back, it's time to examine your sexual history.

Regret comes as a result of pain, shame, and guilt, but it doesn't mean you're locked into a posture of failure and sexual sin. You can know freedom from the stain of past regrets. Christ Jesus will wash you white as snow, but you've got to make an effort.

The only way to fight the darkness is by exposing it to light. Jesus is that light. You must confess your sins of sexual decadence and ask God to forgive you. Along with forgiveness is repentance, which includes changed behavior.

Bringing your regret into healing should also include sharing with someone else. It must be a trusted believer who will not judge you or intensify the hurt you harbor by amplifying the condemnation.

You are also struggling against the binds of soul ties. These are the unseen spiritual connections that create memories and even fantasies of your past sexual experiences with your partners. You must pray over each of these and speak power over them. You have the supernatural authority to cut every soul tie that has shackled you to the painful past.

I once watched as a pastor took a journal where he'd written out his painful sexual history, prayed over it to break the bonds that tormented him for years, and dropped the journal into a fire. He cut those soul ties by forgiving others, praising God, and releasing himself from the destructive nature of sexual regrets.

I assured my friend that she was not a whore, and I also led her to the truth of Jesus Christ. Kind words are like QuikClot on a severed limb. What truly brings healing is the truth of light that repairs the damages done by a life of past sexual sin. The beauty of this is that we know the greatest physician and healer of all—Jesus.

10

MONEY

Big money = big problems, no money = no problems.

Okay, anyone who believes that, just stop reading right here. Money is right up there with kids and sex for the top three culprits that cause fighting and divorce. Added into the mix is that one or both of you are cops, and we're talking high stress jobs with high stakes arguments. Not a good combination at all.

The Elephant in the Room

I'll share that once Leah and I began to discuss marriage, the elephant marched destructively around the room. I'd been a lifelong law enforcement officer. Even at my chief of police's salary, her income as a successful author was considerably more than what I earned.

You'd think a guy would be jumping for joy to have met a wonderful woman raking in that amount of money, but the truth was, I struggled. Maybe it was the man mind, or the alpha ego working overtime, but it played a huge part in our earliest troubles. Or should I say, my earliest troubles.

It's not uncommon for the non-LEO spouse to make more than the

LEO. Many cops marry women who earn more, or they help put their wives through nursing school or other professional studies programs so they can earn more. Suddenly, she's making bank, and her husband is hustling to pick up off-duty details to restore the balance.

Marrying your money isn't about control. It's about submitting to God's model for a relationship based on both people trusting each other with everything they have. But money is a form of dominance we practice over one another. So unless you commit to a shared possession in the most biblical sense of two becoming one, don't expect your money to marry happily.

While Leah and I were preparing for marriage, I wanted to show her how much I loved her, and that income had nothing to do with it. I insisted we sign a prenuptial agreement. I had my pension and earned well, and I wanted her to know she wasn't a supplemental retirement fund. I wanted to do something noble for her.

She was mad as a hornet. I'll explain why in a moment.

One of God's foundational pillars of marriage is the law of partnership/possession. This begins with Adam and Eve, and is still the standard today. When they became one flesh, that extended beyond the physical sex. The two natural people enmeshed into one spiritual, married being. It means that everything you own now also belongs to the other. Let's be real. We like to throw the terms "my" and "mine" around. But the truth is, everything belongs to God. He's blessed us with income, a home, cars, or whatever else we choose to spend HIS money on.

Whether you prosper financially, or just get by paying the bills, you're missing a spiritual blessing by not obeying God's Word to combine everything into one. Once you choose to marry, there can be no *à la carte* of mixing of lives. It's not realistic to say I'll share the bedroom closet, but not your middle child. No, it's all in. When your money is just dating, it may have the tendency to venture out on its own expenditures, new people, or oppress your spouse.

Chances are you earn different salaries, so there is inequity through separate monies. Relational inequity grinds against God's grain. Remember the importance of Genesis: 2:24—two shall become one—

one bank account, one practice of spending and saving, and one in agreement on everything from raises to debt.

You must think in terms of fair, and not equal, when it comes to dealing with every situation that requires money. Will you mix your money, or maintain separate bank accounts? While either plan has the potential to work, it's hard to imagine that managing your own bank account wouldn't lend itself to problems.

Unless there are binding legal contracts, wills, heirs, or annuities preventing the comingling of monies, God's will for the union of two people entering into a heavenly covenant is for two to become one.

Dave Ramsey's *Financial Peace University* is a lifesaver. I don't say that casually because it has made all of the difference in our marriage. There are other resources available, but you must start by asking the question, "Is our money still dating?"

One of Dave's favorite sayings is that if you don't control your money, your money will control you. It'll also take a walk while you're out doing something else. One of the best ways to start practicing disciple stewardship is to tithe from every paycheck. Share ownership of your family's income as an equal partner in its stewardship. This was where Leah's fury was centered when I suggested in the estate planner's office that we sign a prenuptial agreement.

Signing a civil contract instead of focusing on God's marriage covenant wasn't what Leah wanted from me. She wanted my heart to be focused on Christ first and then on her. She was offended, and rightly so. She saw my offer of a prenuptial agreement as an easy out clause. If this marriage doesn't work out at least we'll get to keep what we brought into it.

Yikes. No wonder she was hurt. Our financial security wasn't going to come from a contract, but through Christ.

Here are some great ways to marry your money. We've added a few potential exceptions based on the "fair, not equal" provision.

Combine all money accounts

EXCEPTION—Monies you may have invested, saved for your child's education, elderly care for your parent(s), or other historical investment strategies earmarked for specific interests. For example:

expecting one parent to defund their child's college savings account to pay for the new spouse's child isn't fair. It'll only cause division among parents and siblings.

Work together on developing monthly budgets

Set financial priorities

EXAMPLE—If one spouse has a set retirement, yet the other one wasn't able to dedicate money to a retirement account, make it a joint priority to get that spouse caught up. Look for other opportunities to establish monetary equity for each spouse.

Consult each other before big purchases

Create realistic family financial goals

Discuss money with children in appropriate contexts

EXAMPLE—Blended kids may include one side being accustomed to a level of financial freedoms, while the other side only knew budgets and inabilities to enjoy flexibility. Explaining the shifting financial priority will prepare one side, while assuring the other of fair expectations.

Skip the prenuptials

EXCEPTION—Like I said earlier, unless there are extreme extenuating circumstances, don't prioritize legal agreements on how to work it out in case the marriage fails. Go all in and commit to make the relationship last—cash and all.

Remember, if you're in a blended family, there are two other biological parents with or without resources and expectations.

Remain flexible

Focus on what really matters—1 Timothy 6:10

For the love of money is the root of all evil; and while some have coveted after it, they have erred from the faith and pierced themselves through with many sorrows.

Money is only tough to talk about before you actually decide to start talking about it. Drop the pride and ego before discussing money. It's already a stressful topic, even when there's extra cash brought into the home, so be sensitive. Like learning to shoot center mass, the more you do it, the more natural it becomes. Hit the target on your money's management.

Budgeting

I'm a saver. I grew up as what would be categorized as poor, except that we didn't understand what poor meant. My dad was a public school teacher and coach, and my mom stayed home to raise all seven kids. I had food, clothes, and sugarcane fields to ride my bike through. I often wondered how they pulled it off.

As an adult, I was a cop. A married cop. A dad cop. A divorced cop. A child-support-paying cop. A broke cop. I was poor, and this time I felt it. The cloak of darkness lay over me constantly as I checked and then rechecked my bank accounts to see whether checks had bounced. It was draining the life out of me.

My folks and I were at a local restaurant one night when they flattened out a napkin on the table. My mom pulled out a ballpoint pen and asked how much money I took home each month. Over the next hour, they sketched out the basics of personal finance and budgeting. It was then that I knew how they'd pulled it off. I would give anything to have that napkin as a reminder of how simple the basics of budgeting can be.

Budgets are not battle weapons we form for attacking our spouse. Setting budgets are no more than conversations that reflect your values, goals, needs, and dreams. Of course, conversations that never take place do no one any good. Left in silent speculation, each spouse will come to question each other's intentions.

Money is one of the top three reasons couples fight and divorce. It's usually during the divorce process each of them finally begins to consider the role of money. That's because both are watching it march into their attorneys' pockets.

Let's not do that anymore. It would be such a wonderful accomplishment if we could put divorce attorneys out of business. Don't worry about them, they'll find another way to scrape by! Setting a household budget is vital to the holistic health of your marriage. The stress caused by money is usually a result of failing to control your money. Trust us, if you do not control your cash, your cash will control you.

Taking back control of your money is identifying your money personality. Like I said in the beginning, I'm a saver. Leah is not. There's rarely a sale she can pass up, even if she doesn't need it. Her philosophy is there is someone out there who can use it for that price. And Leah is a giver. She loves to buy things for people or give money. Her spending used to drive me nuts, and until we started budgeting, it caused me to worry nonstop until it had affected my health and our relationship.

Something that also helped us when it came to money was understanding our respective money languages. Once I understood Leah has an Amiable money language and she understood I have a Driver money language, we understood where our hearts were, and understanding your spouse's heart brings clarity to a lot of areas.

What's your money language?

Driver—Money means success, self-esteem, and security.

Amiable—Money means love by buying and sharing to show affection.

Analytic—Money means strength, and keeps away chaos.

Expressive—Money means acceptance and respect as the basis for relationships.

Looking at these types of money languages, you can see how vital each one is for understanding the way we not only think of money, but how it plays an important role in our lives. It's okay if you both practice a different money language, because the variance helps balance the budget. Where the differences are agreed upon is within the context of a written budget. Avoid the debt and the fighting by being proactive in discussing money management through a monthly budget. You might even find you have the extra cash to go do something fantastic for each other.

Leah also grew up poor, but her dad used money to control her and her mom. He never gave out more money than what they needed, and sometimes not even that. His way of showing dominance over his family was to have them come back to him each time, for everything and anything. But instead of Leah developing a saver's language, she used money as a way to show those she loved that her money was their money.

Money can't buy happiness, but it sure can cost you joy. Now is the time to have serious conversations about immediate spending, medium-range objectives like kids, education, vehicles, vacation, and long-term goals such as retirement, a home, or relocating.

The truth is, marriage is good for your finances. There are the tax advantages of course, but the combination of two revenue streams contributing toward a common goal is much more beneficial than working alone, or digging out of the perpetual debt of divorce, alimony, and child support.

Budgeting creates a balanced environment in your marriage, and it allows you both a secure foundation for pursuing other areas of openness and intimacy. There are plenty of ways to begin the conversation about budgeting.

Unless you both are reading this together, one may initially question the motive for bringing up the issue of money management out of the blue. If so, just hold this book up so your spouse can see the next section:

Hi there,

Your spouse is reading our book and this section talks about budgeting money. Trust us, y'all need to have that talk very soon. Like right now. We care about your LEO marriage and can almost guarantee that money worries are already a source of pain in this relationship.

You will both be better off once you begin to control your money instead of allowing your money to control you. Start off by having this talk about setting a budget.

Thanks, and we're praying for you both.

Scott and Leah

Money management can be filled with pitfalls. In addition to the challenge of mismatched spender versus saver philosophies competing for control, there is the bigger issue of spiritual obedience. Now, before you say something about the church not needing your money, we're not here collecting cash for the basket. We want to share several truths about the bigger picture of budgeting.

Tithing and giving isn't about financing some pastor's fancy car. It's about submission and obedience. We also know these terms are contrary to the LEO lifestyle. We're more accustomed to being the one ordering submission and obeying lawful orders. This is where the challenge comes into play, but we will ask that you not allow your current concerns to interfere with an eternal and more meaningful blessing—your marriage.

Failing to manage your money is lacking in a form of stewardship. God does provide, and while we may not think He provides enough after taxes and pension withdrawals, His provision is more than sufficient for what is important in life.

When you neglect honoring Jesus by sharing possession and control of your marriage's money, you place yourself above your spouse in a dominant role, and demote God to second place. Before getting started on a budgeting process, pray that Christ is Lord over your finances and that in giving it up to Him to bless, you both will be blessed with management wisdom.

Another big picture risk with lack of or poor budgeting is the tendency to disrespect your spouse's input on decisions regarding money. How many times have we responded to crime scenes where families fight over money?

Avoid being in that situation from the start by including your spouse in every decision concerning money expenditures. It may be a small amount of cash on the purchase, but it's a huge issue of respect that can be gained and given.

Getting Out of Debt

I'll never forget the month Leah and I spent on our Harley

Davidson touring six thousand miles around the country. It was brutal and beautiful. We were living life out in the open, and loving what America had to offer.

But about halfway into the adventure, my spirit became restless. I waved it off during a twelve-hour ride through the Midwest, somewhere around Montana. I convinced myself it was the devil trying to get into my head about money. Out of nowhere, I started to feel physically ill over the irrational notion that we were in a major financial crisis.

But how could we have been? We'd spent a month in Europe, were on this monster motorcycle trip, and were soon heading to Australia and New Zealand. We had money, and a history of working hard and earning well. No way were we in debt. It had to be the fatigue of the summer sun and handling the big V-twin HOG across rugged mountainous terrain. Oh yeah, and that devil working overtime to get into my head.

After returning home, Leah and I were blindsided by not one, but four lawsuits. This is part of the price you pay when you have a successful business. People will try to take parts of the pie for no reason other than they want what you have. Despite the fact the lawsuits were frivolous, we still had to hire attorneys and see the process through. And attorneys are expensive. We sat at our dining room table, tallying up the potential costs.

We'd both worked hard our entire lives, reaching the top of our respective games and living what we thought was a "blessed" life financially, only to see it completely washed away in a matter of minutes. We'd definitely been blessed, but we weren't good stewards, and though we tithed, there's more to money management than dropping your 10 percent into the plate.

That prompting back on the open roads in the middle of nowhere wasn't fatigue, or road wear, or the devil. It was the Holy Spirit signaling to me that we were in crisis. Not just a little debt, but major, life-changing, destructive debt.

Leah and I had both grown up very simple, but provided for. We'd both advanced in our respective careers so that money wasn't a constant worry. But once we married, we both failed to budget, discuss our different money languages, or plan for a rainy day once. In this instance, our rainy day was hundreds of thousands of dollars in legal fees. We were broke. And for two educated, successful people who looked like they'd taken the world by storm when they married, it was utter humiliation.

It took time, dedication, prayer, and yes, budgeting like we were college kids, eating ramen noodles and hot dogs, before we got a handle on things and worked our way out of the bottomless money hole of attorneys.

If you're in a troublesome financial situation, whether you're a thousand or a million dollars in debt, you know the soul-shattering fear that your world is going to crash down upon you.

I knew going into police work that the money wasn't going to be very much. Sure, there are opportunities for overtime and federal grant work, but the base pay would never land us in the country club.

I've seen this scenario play out thousands of times, and you might be in the middle of it or just coming out of it. Or if you're about to head into it, please stop the cycle. Tell us if this sounds familiar:

- You live with your folks before getting hired by an agency.
- Once hired, you can't be seen living with Mom and Dad, so you get an apartment.
- Of course, your apartment needs furniture and the latest video game system so your new brothers and sisters in blue can hang at your place after shift.
- Your beater car isn't cool enough to park in the department's employee lot, so you buy a big ol' truck. Preferably a black or dark blue truck with rims and dominator wheels. It doesn't matter that you spend most of your time driving a city vehicle.
- The guys aren't coming over like you planned, so you're now spending lots of cash at the bar buying rounds for the brothers.
- Maybe you connect with an old high school flame or

someone you met while working. Dating leads to her moving in, but you're still paying all of the bills.

- You're still a rookie, so premium overtime, grants, and off-duty details go by seniority. You spend your off-duty hours walking up and down the aisles of loss-prevention details trying to get back to the break-even point.
- Within a few months, your live-in girlfriend is gone, you balk on the lease, and you now struggle to pay the balloon note on a truck that spends most of its time in the driveway while you labor in a cruiser trying to scrape by.
- Finally, you work up the nerve to tell the boss there's no way you can be expected to live on what you're being paid. They think to themselves that you knew what the pay was when you accepted the job, and you suspect they are remembering the day you came to work in that big new truck to show off the ten new weapons you bought from the last guy who quit.
- Finally, the neighboring agency is hiring and actually pays more. You quit without notice, blame your co-workers and administration for treating you like a dog, and head out for what amounts to about a quarter an hour more. Even less when you factor the extra distance you have to drive in your POV because of their take-home policy.
- Somewhere between moving back in with the folks, a relative or a few other brothers in the same boat, you decide to get married.

I took a little liberty with the snark because it's the trend I've seen for decades. It was so bad, that as chief of police, I brought in money managers to teach courses to everyone in the department. It immediately helped with attrition and employee motivation.

Living with debt is a horribly dark, oppressive cloud that lurks over every aspect of your life. The worst decisions we can make are those based on fear. So many of us end up quitting law enforcement to find other jobs that pay more per check, but contribute nothing to pension, healthcare, or deferred comp.

We know planning for a thirty-year retirement pension when you're over your head in debt is like giving a drowning man a glass of water, but long-term vision is a part of the process of regaining financial freedom and personal peace.

We're not going to reinvent the wheel. Based on scriptural principles and sound financial management, there are several basic steps that include a commitment to take control of your money. Don't be afraid of money. It will only hurt you when you don't take control. Money also has a way of walking away unless you have a firm grip on it. This isn't being stingy, it's about survival.

Whether our rookie year example rang true with you or not, the reality is not that we don't make enough money. The problem is that we spend too much money. Take a look at our Debt Rescue 911 Plan. It saved us, and we know it can save you too.

Debt Rescue 911

The idea of debt can be overwhelming, especially when it feels like you're drowning. Believe me, we've been there too. We know that cops are underpaid and overworked. We also know from experience that our life choices often make things like financial planning or debt more difficult.

Get a notepad, or better yet, use the debt and budget worksheets at the back of this book and write down every debt you have. Every. Single. One. No matter how big or how small. Take deep breaths while doing this because if you've never tallied every single one of your obligations, you're going to feel very lightheaded, if not physically sick.

Do not panic. The only way to heal from darkness is by shining light on it. This list of debt is going to be your light because you've finally exposed what you've ignored or hidden until a crisis was at hand. Once they're down on paper you know exactly what you need to tackle. Pay off the smallest debts first.

What can you cut? It's time to reprioritize and focus on the things that matter. You need a roof over your head, utilities, food, and transportation. Those are the most important things. Pay those bills first every month. Your A+ credit rating isn't going to mean much if you get evicted for not paying the rent.

Do you have a $600 per month car note? Do you have two car notes? Getting out of debt requires sacrifice, and sometimes that means you can't drive the best truck or car. Get rid of those car payments. Trade your vehicles in on something that is completely paid for. Even if it's a junker. It's a temporary fix to get you back on track. You'll have a nicer car again before you know it because this time you'll have planned and saved for it.

What else can you cut? How about cable? Or expensive phone plans? There was a time in our marriage where we had to get rid of everything but the basic necessities. Are you getting the best rates for car insurance? Have you even checked to compare? This is an area that can sometimes save you several hundred dollars a year.

Do you eat out while on shift? Is restaurant life your way of living? Eating out is one of the biggest areas where we throw money away. It's the same thing with those trips to Starbucks for an extra shot of caffeine when you're on hour eight of a twelve-hour shift. Five dollars a day for coffee adds up to $1,825 a year. That would go a long way in paying down debt.

Start couponing. And make your shopping lists and meals for the week based on what's on sale, or what you have coupons for.

Are you paying for a gym membership you rarely or never use? Time to cut it from your expenses. You can jog in your neighborhood for free. What about expensive hobbies like golf? It's a good time to take a break. The golf clubs will still be there when you're out of debt and can afford the tee fees.

Getting out of debt takes determination and a mindset that you're going to win. According to 2017 data, the average American household has more than $137,000 in debt, yet the average household income is only $56,000.

You can do it. We know it's possible because we did it. You'll be surprised where you can find extra money to put toward your debts so you can be 100 percent debt free. Is the money from off-duty details going toward debt or next year's vacation? Vacation is even better when you don't come home broke.

What can you sell? Have a garage sale, or sell items on social media marketplaces to bring in some extra cash, and then put that cash toward debt.

It's important to use the budget sheet every month. Don't just fill it out, but follow it. Use the cash you have to live within your means. That means no credit cards to fall back on! And start putting every extra cent you have toward paying off the smallest debts first. We tell you to pay off the smallest debts first because it feels good to succeed quickly. Once you pay off that debt (say, for example, you pay $68 per month on a TV until it's paid off), that money can now go toward your next lowest debt.

We're not saying this is going to be your way of life forever, or that you should never have fun. That's what the budget sheet is for. Fun is a lot more...well...fun if you know exactly what you can spend without the threat of your electricity being cut off. If there's something special you want to do, or a special occasion coming up, just budget for it and stick to it.

Guess what? This really is you and your spouse against the world, and if you don't watch each other's six, the bill collector is going to take it all. But you're both fighters and willing to roll up your sleeves and dig into the fray for as long as it takes to pull yourselves out of the dread of debt.

Please don't ever give up on regaining your financial freedom. The average debt takes almost two years to pay off if you follow the plan to the letter. It may seem impossible, but when you're drawing close to your spouse and taking control of what was a bad situation, you begin to experience a sense of control over the fear of debt. Soon, you're making that last payment and enjoying the new lease on your marriage's financial life. Most importantly, pray about your finances and discuss them openly with your spouse. God will bless your faithfulness.

Give and Get

Leah and I weren't able to make church one weekend because a few of the kids were sick. We sat on the couch watching it online instead. Both of us were still in shock over the insurmountable debt looming over our heads. Guess what the message was about—giving.

Honestly, that was the last thing I wanted to hear about. I mean, really, how in the world would we even scrape two pennies together, much less give to the church? I felt a spirit of anger sweep over me and I got up off of the couch. Fear was still in my soul, and although we faithfully tithed through the darkest of our debt, I wasn't going to give one penny more. Like I said, it was fear, but I was allowing it to make me angry and resentful.

Leah lovingly suggested that we stop playing it safe, and show our faith in God's promise to provide. We'd stashed away one thousand dollars just in case of an emergency, and she wanted us to give that money as an offering. I might've initially laughed or yelled. I can't be sure, but no matter my reaction, it wasn't one I'm proud of.

We're cops. That means we're capable of getting things done no matter what getting it done looks like. We're self-reliant, self-sufficient, and yes, at times, selfish. My blue line pride was preventing me from a major blessing and breakthrough. I knew God's faithful promise and how often He came through for us, but in that moment, I was a prisoner to the fear of letting go of that emergency fund.

The second I began to pray, not about the one thousand dollars, but about why I was so afraid, God began to soften my heart about the message of giving.

We invest in a volatile stock market with hopes of return, scratch off a lottery ticket in hopes of a payout, or feed cash into a slot machine with the expectation of a jackpot. So why are we faithless and fearful about investing in the only 100 percent return on our submission and obedience?

This truth will serve you well when faced with debt or major financial decisions: go for God instead of gold in all that you do, and while you're both at it, please understand that debt is often a condition of our faith, and not our finances.

Here are seven poverty pitfalls, and God's Word as evidence:

1. Laziness

Contrary to popular belief, labor/work isn't punishment from God (*Proverbs 24:30–31*). Anyone ever associated with law enforcement knows this because we work harder than anyone I know. But when facing financial difficulties, we tend to hoard our cash and efforts instead of giving the extra push to work for more opportunity.

2. Oversleeping

We know it takes certain amounts of sleep to remain healthy, but most cops are plagued by chronic fatigue. Thanks to long shifts, overtime, and investigations that seem to never end, we suffer from a lack of regular rest. It is because of this disruptive work cycle that when we do have free time, it's spent asleep. Beyond normal, healthy recovery sleep, becoming a couch zombie is akin to laziness and yet another poverty pitfall (*Proverbs 20:13*).

3. Stinginess

Looking at *Proverbs 11:24–25*, we know what it is to be stingy, and it's what we are talking about by giving to get. You will never, ever out give God. Anne Frank famously said, "No one has ever become poor by giving."

4. Unteachable Spirit

I used to resent the "older" cops at in-service trainings. Their smugness was an insult to the trainers who gave their time and talent to teach us the latest in law, policy, or survival. The truth was, it served no point for those guys to even show up. They had an unteachable spirit. They were still going to write bad arrests reports, violate regs, and fumble with yanking their revolvers out of a nylon holster.

When God is working on you through the Holy Spirit, please don't become one of the unteachable (*Proverbs 13:18*). Be open and sensitive to His work in your life. There is a blessing just waiting for your attentiveness.

5. Addiction

Remember the rookie life example that led to poverty? It's not uncommon for cops or their spouses to develop job-related addictions or compulsive behaviors that are health risks and financially devastating.

Studies show that academy cadets who have never smoked are likely to start smoking just to fit in with the other cadets who smoke. It goes the same for abusing alcohol. Surrendering control of your body and will to external influences shows a lack of discipline and interferes with God's work in your life (*Proverbs 23:21*).

6. Birds of a Feather: Worthless People or Pursuits

Show me your friends, and I'll show you your future.

Leah and I began a practice of looking at the people in our lives and making decisions about how much of our time we would give them, if any at all. Now, some people take that as being "un-Christian," selfish, and a whole myriad of not nice names.

The truth is, we don't care. Your job as a LEO means you are at the beck and call of everyone, all the time. Even as the top cop, my time wasn't my own. In our marriage, we must protect the precious time we have together. Be intentional who you decide to gift with your time and attention.

The jokers in your squad might be reliable when the stuff hits the fan, but their third divorce and sixth kid do nothing to mentor your relationship with your spouse. Wealth is built over consistent effort and focus. Avoid those who cause you to take your eye off of the prize (*Proverbs 28:19*).

7. Greed and Covetousness

Like all of God's Word, *Proverbs 28:20–22* is profound. Whether it was listed in the bible or a business manual, it's pretty solid advice. If your sole focus is making rank instead of serving others, your career will languish in dissatisfaction. Pursuing earthly wealth ironically leads to poverty.

Don't allow the fear of finances or a temporary debt to cause you to cut corners or compromise who you are. You and your spouse are one in this, and by coveting money or material things, you instantly relegate them below whatever it is you desire. This violates God's law of priority in placing Him first and your gift of a spouse next. Keep that straight and you'll hit the mark

For what shall it profit a man, if he shall gain the whole world, and lose his own soul?
Mark 8:36

I almost forgot. That day I was so upset over the preacher's message about giving above and beyond tithes, things could've gone either way for me. It was the prayers that gave me peace and the insight to understand that clinging on to a thousand dollars wasn't going to get us out of a lot of thousands of dollars of debt. It was going to be our faith that carried us through.

We gave that money, knowing full well that we had a huge obligation hanging immediately over our heads. I know you hear these testimonies all the time, so I'm a little hesitant to share ours. But that very same week we gave, we received three big lump sum payments from the most random and unexpected sources imaginable.

Although the three sums didn't even scratch the surface of our total debt, the exact dollar amount of the three separate sources equaled the precise total of what was pressing upon us to be paid at the time. Faith is taking one step into the dark and trusting God to shine His light just before our foot falls. He lights our path in life, love, and yes, even finances.

11

COMMUNICATIONS

Let's kick off this chapter with a reminder—men and women are different. We were created different by design, and we will always be different by intention. Part of that difference is reflected in the way we communicate with each other.

If you've been in law enforcement for more than a week, our bet is that you already blend your speech with your agency's ten-code. Leah understands the lingo, ten-codes, and the disposition signals. When the other cops and I had modified status calls into something only insiders understood, Leah knew exactly what was going down.

Sure, it's a bonding thread, just like any other occupation adapts the speech of their employment, and it's fun to share with your spouse. I recall being a kid, slicing through the tall sugarcane stalks of south Louisiana. We had adopted a mash-up of English, creole French, and some Spanish slang to enjoy a secret-coded talk that even our parents didn't understand.

Chances are, you and your spouse have your own language. Maybe some of it is silent cues, disapproving glances, impatient snorts of exhaled air, or a subtle nod of the chin in affirmation. Leah and I even planned tactical comms before heading into family and public events so we'd know when it was time to ramp up, wrap up, or head out.

But in the daily grind of fleeting hellos and hurried goodbyes, we miss important opportunities for communicating with each other in meaningful ways. This is where the differences between us become obvious and often confrontational.

Rare is the good, solid marriage that isn't grounded in positive communications. LEOs get so used to keeping talk brief to avoid tying up the police radio or avoid giving too much away during a defense attorney's cross examination, that when it comes time for opening up to their spouse, they remain a closed book.

Social media is altering the way we communicate. It's not just for kids, because married couples rely on texting when they don't have time to talk, or when they'd rather avoid a face-to-face confrontation. We know a couple that claimed texting helped save their marriage because they used to fight every time they started talking.

We're not sure that's a solid long-term strategy, but chances are it's only prolonging what will soon become a major blowout. When it happens, and it will happen, they'll find themselves without a solid foundation for talking through their issues.

Communicating is how we actually get to know each other. Think back to when you first met. How many hours did you spend talking with each other, clinging on to every word? It was critical for learning about each other, and mostly it was fun. We're willing to bet that you both used lots of positive talk and active listening so you wouldn't miss a single detail.

So what happened? You're both still interesting people, and beyond the initial physical attractions, love has become a fixture in the relationship. The difference is you are no longer sharing through communications. Talking about house chores, paying bills, and work doesn't count.

Intimate, vulnerable conversations are what cement marriages. If you both have fallen into a rut of only covering the surface in your conversations, or default to negative and cutting words, please know that you can turn it around.

From the fruit of their mouth a person's stomach is filled;
with the harvest of their lips they are satisfied.
The tongue has the power of life and death,
and those who love it will eat its fruit.
Proverbs 18:20–21

We may not realize the power of each spoken word, but the soul does. It's either uplifted or cut clean to the core. In law enforcement, we encounter people who, by the very nature of what they say, may be understood as a threat against our wellbeing. They are charged with a criminal offense. Yet when we use the very same context or tone toward our wife, we don't consider the severity of what was said against them.

Your spouse is not the enemy or some street-level confrontation. Married couples should not measure individual successes by arguments won and lost. Both lose when arguments become the standard. Forgiveness, affirmation, and understanding will help you avoid the marital autopsy.

Can we take a moment to go back to Proverbs 18:20–21? Sometimes we get in a rush and brush over bible verses when they're ones we're familiar with. But this is so profound that its implications should stop us in our tracks.

Some people think it's just a metaphor that words hold the power of life and death, but consider the actual, literal reality that someone can pronounce that you physically are allowed to live, or be put to death. Not such a metaphor now. In a spiritual realm, the tongue either affirms another with positive words, or the death can be the killing of hope, peace, joy, or love.

Wasted words also have eternal consequences. We think that if couples could witness this holy judgment like we watch in episodes of *Live PD*, there would be fewer negative, hurtful words spoken to each other.

While we're thinking through Proverbs, please review everything you've said to your wife in the last twenty-four hours. How about the last twelve hours, or more realistically, the last few hours. How would you be judged (*Matthew 12:36–37*)—condemned or acquitted?

Just as we learn the laws as to not break them, we too can learn or relearn to speak positive, affirming words to our spouse. When we truly see our spouse in the context of God's foundational laws of marriage: priority, possession, pursuit, and purity—there is no desire to withhold positive communications.

I thought my parents had the perfect marriage. They never fought, were always together, and made themselves available to all seven kids. When I married, the fantasy of never fighting, always being together, and making ourselves available to our son was just that—a fantasy. Actually, it became a nightmare, which eventually turned into a divorce.

When Leah and I married, it began again. I just knew I'd made a mistake in marrying her because we started to have arguments, weren't available for each other all the time, and there was no way to be everywhere for everyone. It was a dark time. After waiting almost twenty years for God to bless me with a wife, did I misread His will? Of course not.

What I had misread was the reality that my parents did not have a perfect marriage. They had a marriage like anyone who was willing to dig in and stick it out, no matter what came their way. What I had missed in the bliss of youth was that they fought, were absent, and sometimes we kids didn't get to ball practice on time.

Leah and I quickly came to understand we needed to learn how to fight fair. She is a peacekeeper, and I'm genetically geared toward dominating a situation by force of personality. I'm not saying I have a stellar one, but it's a character trait that I've been aware of as long I can recall. Whether it was drawing plays in the dirt with a stick before we scored a touchdown as the streetlights kicked on, or negotiating a felon out of a barricaded standoff, I'm obsessed with getting it done, no matter the cost or consequences.

Honestly, it was and sometimes remains a struggle to put away my police command voice in the heat of an argument with Leah. And if you also have a dominant personality, don't fool yourself into thinking that your spouse knows better than to be afraid or hesitant in how they respond to the things you say and the way you say them.

If you fail to provide your spouse with a safe place to fight, then they'll avoid the ring. Their avoidance doesn't signal your victory or understanding. It means they've been defeated, and that is never a good posture for your partner in this life. To borrow a saying from our friend Pastor Dave Willis, "A husband and wife must function like two wings on the same bird. They must work together in partnership or the marriage will never get off the ground."

The biggest single change in the way we spoke to each other was the morning we began praying together. It was a tough road for me to arrive at the place of being able to pray with Leah. I had a faithful and deep prayer life on my own, but the reality was, no one spouse can be completely whole in prayer life without their other equal half. So the day I stopped operating at half capacity was the day prayer time changed my life.

We're cops, and by the authority of our commission and the grace of God, we are in charge of "policing" society. I say that with a grin because although some in society may disagree, the truth as we know it is everyone in America is subject to some form of law. And because of our position, we're there to make sure it's adhered to. So do you see the conflict between shifting roles from regulator to the regulated?

Praying together was tough for me because I was resistant to being vulnerable in front of my wife. By the way, that is the only way we may come before God. Carrying pride, arrogance, cockiness, or general 'tude to the altar will get us shot down every time.

Praying together will show you the right way to communicate with God, and after all, the relationship with our wife was mirrored in the way He communicates with us. Therefore, praying together serves as a mentoring session with the ultimate marriage coach.

An added bonus to praying together is that we begin to ask forgiveness and apologize to our spouses instead of taking pride in getting the last dig in. When we stop keeping score, and recalling past wounds through hurtful words, we begin treating our spouse like the gift God gave us.

A gentle answer turns away wrath,
but a harsh word stirs up anger.
Proverbs 15:1

Here are a few ways to make sure you both fight fair:

- Start your sentences with "I" instead of "You"—"I feel frustrated when we're late" is easier to hear than "You always make us late."
- Keep your fighting away from your kids unless you model how to resolve it in front of them.
- Stay clear of "character assassination"—don't assign negative labels to each other (e.g. "You're so lazy").
- If you need a time-out, take it, but agree on when you'll come back.
- Avoid expressing contempt by rolling your eyes or being sarcastic. It's toxic to your relationship.

Not Pleading the Fifth

"Just back off."

I'll confess I barked that at Leah after one of many tough times on the job. She immediately deflated before my eyes. The exhausted but bright, smiling face that had worried over me during the extended hours of a homicide callout, now looked defeated.

I was so exhausted from the hours and gruesomeness of the scene that I pushed past her and sat in my regular hard-back wooden chair. Thus began one of many silent treatment dances we played when the reality of the job became too real to just be a job.

I knew she'd walked off, but I continued to sit there in full uniform and remained quiet. I soon heard my wife, who rarely sheds a tear, crying in the back room. But I was too numb, and by that time, too agitated. Why didn't she understand I only wanted silence?

It wasn't fair then, and it's not fair now if you're doing this same kind of silent treatment over not wanting to communicate, versus their need to connect with you. When I'm in the mood for sex and she just wants to hang out, I feel rejected. So why is it any different when it comes to communication?

LEOs must learn to exist in the push-pull world of communicating with precision, yet tailoring conversations to protect confidentiality. It's a balancing act that some master, while others fumble. Because of my twelve years working undercover drugs and violent crimes, I tended to lean toward the adage of the less said the better.

While that's fine for the job, it's an unacceptable way to withhold from your wife. This also overlaps into daily life. Actually, it becomes the pattern for the duration of your marriage. When difficulties arise, we'll find ourselves unwilling or unable to talk it through. Thanks to pleading the Fifth on everything from what you want for your birthday to why you no longer want to make love, it will continue to drive your spouse away.

We all have the desire to connect through relationship. Married couples are blessed to have the most important person on this earth as their anchor. This is why, of all the people we choose to shut down in front of, our spouse cannot be that person. No way can you share a life, but not a talk. Don't clam up. Just like God, they need to hear what's on your heart and in your head.

Let's get spiritual about this. The devil loves it when you go silent. It's the very same tactic he used to cause the fall of man. It was just Adam and Eve in paradise, but we tend to think of Eve being caught alone in the garden when satan approached her. But check this out:

When the woman saw that the fruit of the tree was good for food and pleasing to the eye, and also desirable for gaining wisdom, she took some and ate it. She also gave some to her husband, who was with her, and he ate it.
Genesis 3:6

Adam was right there! Satan found a way to slip in between the only two people who have ever experienced a perfect marriage, and he tempted her. But Adam wasn't engaged with his wife through communication. Had he been, he would've run that serpent out of the garden. Instead, there had been silence, and the devil knew it was his time to move. It's easy to get complacent and go through the "routine" of life without checking in on each other. We've all been there, done that. But it's these times of separation and lack of communication where it's easy for the devil to slip in.

What's waiting to invade your relationship?

Refusing to talk with your spouse isn't as much about needing to decompress as you tell yourself. That's an excuse. It's about manipulation, and it can turn into into a form of psychological abuse. While you're still in the same home, silence can be one of the cruelest forms of emotional abandonment.

When suspicions arise over anything from finances to affairs, pleading the Fifth only serves you well in court, and might very well end you up there—divorce court. Patterns are easy to establish and very tough to break. One of you setting the tone that silence will be the way to non-handle challenges leaves the ignored spouse with few options for resolving serious issues.

On a few last notes, we are designed for relationships. If one of you goes radio silent and leaves the other one yearning for the relationship for which we were created, it's not uncommon for them to seek satisfaction elsewhere. We're not saying it's right, but we are saying it's common.

Here are a few tactics for dealing with a spouse who pleads the Fifth like a mob boss testifying before congress:

If one of you decides you need a time of silence or to decompress, then inform your spouse you need this time, but reassure them that you'll come back around to the conversation later. Your spouse will understand.

If you're the spouse being shut out, don't respond with threats or agitating gestures.

Understand ahead of time that silence is a control tactic to avoid furthering the topic, scaring you into dropping the subject, or avoiding confession or apology.

If silence comes at the peak of anger, don't poke the bear on principle. Allow a cooling off before insisting that the conversation resumes.

Don't wait until the silent treatment begins to know how it will be handled. An ounce of prevention is worth a pound of cure.

The one thing that neither of you want to do is to accept or convince each other that you're married to the strong silent type. Breaking the silence only takes a little effort and a few words. Usually "I'm sorry" works wonders.

Pillow Talk

It's funny how I like to go face-to-face when it's time for Leah and me to engage in what we call "spirited fellowship." In case you've never heard that term, that's what we call an argument. But our most intimate and vulnerable talks happen while we're lying shoulder to shoulder in bed.

I think guys are most comfortable talking while they're either doing something, watching something, or pretending to be preoccupied with something. Maybe that's why guys talk while sitting at a bar watching the game on TV. It's a way of being engaged and still disassociated from a posture of vulnerability by having to face emotions from the other person.

As we were prepping this section, Leah laughed when I told her my concept of "pillow talk" was supposed to be sexy and flirtatious and lead to...well, sex. Leah said no way. Apparently, pillow talk isn't sexual. Who knew? Her idea of pillow talk is when you're lying in bed and just...gasp...talk.

So we agreed to compromise. But the truth is, good communication builds intimacy, and intimacy leads to other things. Yes, even sex. Whether the talk is about something playful or serious, women must never, ever disclose anything shared by their husband.

If a man feels his words are smeared and trust betrayed, that will be the last time he opens up. It's difficult for a man to be vulnerable and share his feelings. Don't betray him by sharing his dreams, goals, struggles, or frustrations with your mom, best girlfriends, or social media.

On the other side of the pillow, a woman's words flow more freely. While she doesn't require you to sign a nondisclosure agreement, every word shared between spouses should always be kept between them.

Now that trust is set as a communication priority, let's talk about the way we talk. Women are more emotion based. Some say that as a bad thing, but it's possibly why women live longer than us guys. Feelings and emotions are big influencers in life, and the woman most in touch with hers has a major advantage in expressing herself once she knows there is a safe place to land in the marriage communication model.

While women speak the language of love and security, men speak the language of honor and respect. Both are willing to veer off track just a bit, but the reality is, for each to fully feel equal and accepted as a participant in the pillow talk, each responds to their respective language.

Phrases from you like, "I care and I'll do whatever it takes," are so important to your wife. Meanwhile, husbands seek affirmation through phrases like, "I believe in you, or I trust you." Simple, sincere encouragements are as effective as your work partner whispering, "Let's roll," just before kicking in a door.

No matter what your pillow talk sessions evolve into, please never assume your spouse knows what's on your mind or your heart. Direct lines of communications are vital in the fight for marriage.

Just think about how lost you'd be without your police dispatchers. We call them our lifelines for a reason. It's not that they cover us in gunfire, or fight for us in a brawl, but they make sure we get the help or relief needed. It's no different at home. You must keep those lines open.

MarriageToday's founder, Pastor Jimmy Evans, has these tips for successful communication:

1. Care—You can't communicate with a person who doesn't care.
Be careful in your body language, countenance, and tone of voice.
Be a good listener.

Give a kind and appropriate response.

2. Praise—We have to begin with a positive tone.

We enter into each other's heart with praise. (Psalm 100:4)

Say negative things in a positive way. Negativity destroys marriages.

3. Truth—Honesty is an essential foundation of intimacy and trust.

We need mercy and truth. (Proverbs 3:3)

Speak the truth in love. (Ephesians 4:15)

4. Faith—Believe that God is able to enforce the truth in your spouse's heart.

Women can change their husbands with actions instead of words.

A gentle and quiet spirit means that you have faith in God and won't try to be the enforcer.

Once you speak the truth in love, pray and believe God for the results.

5. Surrender—Decide that your mouth is God's mouth and is dedicated to serving and glorifying Him.

12

TOXIC RELATIONSHIPS

Pruning Toxic Exes

We used to think it was only the holidays that brought out the worst in people. Okay, when we say *people* we're talking about ex-spouses or the biological parent of your child. This may be the only time we're going to try to be "PC" and use the term *people*.

The truth is, as a LEO family, you come under constant attack from exes, in-laws, friends, families, community, and sometimes, each other. The levels of toxicity in law enforcement are what drive us to an early grave.

This is why we want you both to focus on this chapter. If you have to walk up to the two-yard line on the range to make sure you rip right through the bull's-eye to get this chapter right, then do it, but do not miss the mark.

The people who are toxic in your life, and also have leverage in injecting misery, will seldom change their hearts or their motives. We're not talking about the ex who wants to get the kids back an hour early on a school night. We're referring to those people who are shrouded in misery.

There's a German word, *schadenfreude*, that I learned early in my career as others took constant shots at my life's light. It helped me to articulate exactly what these types of people are so that I could reclaim power into my life. It literally means deriving pleasure from the misfortunes of others. In German, it is "harm-joy," and like so many people we know, they sit like crows on a wire waiting to enjoy failure or suffering in others while happily dropping their own poop bombs on our life whenever they can.

The beauty of recognizing this is that you now have the spiritual authority to release yourself from them. How do you protect your current spouse, the children you and your ex share, the children you and your current spouse have, and anyone else in the blended familial mix?

Exes who were toxic during the relationship or marriage don't necessarily remain toxic after divorce. The conditions of a failing marriage may have been the cause of their poor behavior. There are really no true red flags that predict or preclude toxic behavior, but there is behavior to remain watchful for that illustrates toxicity.

Prepare yourself, and avoid unhealthy confrontations. While your current spouse should be aware of the history and all current issues, your children should not be subjected to an unhealthy or potentially unsafe environment.

Exes are a source of marital strife and eventual divorce if the external influence isn't handled effectively. Marriage counselors share that portions of counseling sessions are dedicated to equipping one or both parties with the tools required to resist the toxic ex's manipulation and control tactics.

How to Identify a Toxic Ex:

This section isn't for everyone. You might be on great terms with your ex, but here's a few ways to identify problems if your post-relationship terms aren't so great.

Do they have an unrealistic expectation for accessing you and your children at will? Does your phone ring at mealtimes and bedtimes? Or do FaceTime calls become your ex's invasive surveillance mission inside your home?

Setting boundaries is a priority to save your marriage and your sanity. Set scheduled call times, and restrict where the kids may sit to FaceTime or Skype with their other parent. Your child may not realize they're being manipulated, but it's not uncommon for the other parent to use a video calling as a tool to interject themselves into your family through their voice over an open speaker or their image displayed to you, your spouse, and the other kids.

"Show me Mommy's or Daddy's new car," may seem innocent, but it may also be yet another way of building ammunition to use in future battles with you. Short of sticking your child inside a broom closet, it's best to limit their roaming capabilities.

Interrogations

The toxic ex has the misconception they are the only one capable of parenting the child. The child's time with you is merely a distraction until baby is back home with the real parent. The ex feels empowered to grill you over the time the child has spent away from them.

It's disguised by acts of interests in activities or time shared, but be cautious about what information is revealed. It's not only a tactic used to make you recount your actions, but it's a control mechanism for directing your actions in the future.

Sabotage

I know it's sounding more like a counter-terror operation than a parenting piece, but we're talking about toxic exes who would be just as happy with destroying your current marriage as they would doubling your child support, while cutting your visitation in half.

The toxic ex isn't your acute complainer. They are chronic, strategic, and relentless. Many spouses do not see the manipulative power influencing them or their shared children. Once the current spouse attempts to assist in managing the invasion, they are often met with resistance or resentment. This is the goal of the toxic ex.

While they may not want you running back into their arms, they sure don't want you in a healthy new marriage. Beware the saboteur!

Hearts and Minds

Many courts use the boilerplate custody verbiage "Alienation of Affection." This simply means one parent shall not turn the child against the other parent. Remain mindful of what the child says. They are parrots and repeat what they hear.

Active listening helps you to understand what the toxic ex is feeding the child's mind with, and often what words are being used by the ex to describe you to your child.

It's not always the goal of the toxic ex to terminate your rights of custodial visitation. Many exes don't want the added burden of more time or responsibilities associated with childcare as it interferes with their personal, adult time with friends or a new mate.

The goal among most of these manipulators is they want you to fail in the act of raising the shared child, so you become dependent on the "one true parent" —the toxic ex. It's about exerting control. Control over you.

Damn the Torpedoes

Statistically, more dads take mothers to court over interference in visitation than mothers take dads to court for nonpayment of child support. While that might be deciphered to show men are more prone to initiate court action, it does illustrate that there's a problem on both sides with neither parent abiding by the court's decree relative to custodial visitations.

The toxic ex could care less about what court papers say. They know it back and forth, and only rely upon it when it suits their needs. Seldom do parents rely solely upon a child custody agreement without ever making exceptions or provisions on the fly. While this is usually done with the child's best interest, it's also a trap to be aware of. Ever found yourself muttering, "Yeah, but last time…?"

I'm sure you know as well as I do that seldom will a law enforcement agency get involved in interfering with the civil process concerning child visitation. Officers are called into custody disputes more often than they're called to armed robberies. The high majority of agencies will never remove a child from one parent and award to the other parent unless there is a directed court order specifying that action be taken by an officer.

We're sharing this because of a few reasons. Don't wrongly assume your position as a LEO will afford you extra courtesies or protections. Often, it's used against you, and although you may be tempted to do so, please don't use the badge to coerce what's not in the decree.

Most men are guilty of blowing off the toxic ex's behavior as no big deal. And burying your head in the sand might work for a while. But it becomes a big problem when you remarry or have new children. If you value the sanctity of your new marriage, or just your own peace of mind, then give this the attention it deserves.

While it's vital to be objective and not label someone as toxic because of their displeasure over you running an hour late, it is critical to monitor the toxic ex's behavior and attempts at destructive tactics. It's more than a once or twice intrusion. If not addressed immediately, it will become the pattern of your life. It also has the destructive power to end your current marriage.

Ten Tips for Coping with the Toxic Ex:

1. Acknowledge your role in the ongoing conflict.
2. Don't use the badge to intimidate the ex. It tarnishes the shield and always comes back to haunt you.
3. If you must discuss anything with an ex, make sure it's impersonal to avoid excessive conflict.
4. Preplan or write out talking points to guide through typically emotional negotiations.

5. Whenever possible, give a little to get a little. No one wants to walk away empty-handed.
6. If the discussion is about shared children, only talk about the shared children.
7. It's natural for kids to become confused or angry with the other biological parent. Do not use this as a wedge to drive them apart. This pendulum swings both ways.
8. Loyalty and loss are hurtful to the kids. Don't make them choose sides.
9. Forgive like Christ on the cross.
10. Even if you have to bite your tongue, be respectful of the ex's authority over the child and their own life.

Pruning Toxic In-Laws

The best way to convey this section is to share our story and the pain it caused in our marriage. Leah is an only child. Raised by her grandparents, there was no extended family for a young girl to love and enjoy in her small Texas town. My dad left his family in Philadelphia and moved south where he remained the rest of his entire life. Our family never knew grandparents, cousins, uncles, or aunts until we became adults and discovered them. My mom's family were also from another state. Just like Leah, we were isolated. Except we had seven kids in our family.

When we met, she was so excited that I came from a big Italian family. I knew it was one of the draws of our relationship, and I was so excited to share that with her. Her kids had no cousins or extended family. They too were amped up at the idea of having a bunch of aunts, uncles, and cousins. It was familial heaven.

Except that it wasn't. My sisters have always treated girlfriends and wives like second-class citizens. Usually worse. Actually, they openly referred to them not as in-laws, but outlaws. One of my sisters-in-law has been married to my brother over thirty-five years, and she has been treated as an outcast every day for no other reason than hatefulness.

Of course, the way generational iniquities travel, my sister's daughters also have a healthy dose of disrespect for anyone not of Silverii blood. Leah was devastated at first discovery, but she tried her best to play it honest and open about how they made her feel. That was like pouring gas on a dumpster fire.

Oddly enough, the same family members who took the greatest pride in my being chief of police, were also the ones who openly expressed their disgust at my retirement. Why? Because they are selfish consumers of other people. I could no longer do anything for them, or through position, give them social influence. Of course, these examples were just tips of the iceberg. Our family carries deep pain from generational dysfunction, so it wasn't as though love was the thread that stitched us together. We were a very dysfunctional family.

There were other devastating life choices my sisters made, and despite the blood shared between us, we decided their actions and behavior were harmful to us, my other siblings, and our children. Blood is not thicker than water.

Eventually, Leah and I prayed over the decision to prune these joy-sucking forces from our life. It was hard. Very hard. But when Leah and I looked at the darkest areas of stress between us, and areas that caused us to fight or just live in misery, it was traced directly back to their negative influences in our life. Pruning relationships isn't easy, but it may become necessary. There's biblical foundations, and practical applications, for protecting your marriage.

What is a toxic in-law or family relationship? Well, look at what we just shared for a great example. Does it mean you have to cut them off completely? No, not always, but pruning can also refer to cutting back.

It's natural for in-laws to conflict with new spouses while everyone is adjusting to the new dynamic. But if the conflict continues or the environment becomes hostile and manipulative, you're in a toxic scenario.

A toxic relationship is about control and is a habitual condition that extends beyond the purview of the newness of a new family member through marriage. They are chronic, strategic, and relentless in their pursuit for reclaiming control over their family member. It may not be purposeful at first, but once confronted about the hurt they cause, it should stop. If they don't—it's toxic.

You might have already experienced this, but it's not uncommon for a toxic in-law to join forces with the toxic ex. Birds of a feather really do flock together, or maybe more appropriate, misery loves company.

The foundational rock upon which marriage is based looks to the very first marriage covenant between Adam and Eve. It's called the Leave and Cleave Clause.

Therefore shall a man leave his father and his mother, and shall cleave unto his wife: and they shall be one flesh.
Genesis 2:24

God says nothing about parents or in-laws as part of that meshing into one. Just as it would be unnatural for you to include someone else in your marriage, so it goes for your parents and in-laws. Remember back in the blended family section when we said raising your kids is a temporary assignment, but marriage was designed to last forever? This is where it really hits home with practical application.

Your parents have completed their mission of raising you once you've become an adult. Even if you lived in the spare room a few extra years. But now that you've married, you really are an adult and no longer your parents' or siblings' responsibility.

Sometimes parents have trouble letting go. That is why God said a man shall leave his mother and father... That is an active term, not lingering between being married to your spouse while clinging to Mommy.

Your spouse must be the singularly most important person on this earth. Also, it cannot be kept a sweet secret between the two of you. Let me go back to my brother and wife of so many decades. He always has and continues to make it known that he will always side with his wife. He's never spoken ill of her to his siblings or my parents, and when it came down to being forced to make a choice, he sided with his wife. You can image how that went over, but guess what, they're still married thirty-five years strong!

It's the same way in policing—the fastest way to fail is trying to please everyone. Some will get the warning, while some get the cuffs. Focus on pleasing your wife first. Even if you disagree with her, have that conversation away from an audience and support her in front of others. Wives, always do the same for your husband.

Don't give your in-laws tickets to the sideshow. Phone calls to family criticizing your spouse empowers family to try and "fix it" or interject. And by fixing it, that also includes taking sides or possibly even suggesting divorce. If you want family out of your marriage, be careful how often you invite them in.

If your in-laws know as much about your relationship as you do, then there's a problem between you and your spouse. They shouldn't know each argument, major purchases, child issues, or any other private matter that goes on in the sanctity of your home.

Forgiveness between a husband and wife should become a continuing process. But parents and families tend to hold on to offenses against their loved one. We've seen parents bring up food tabs from the wedding reception twenty years later. In-laws were not part of God's marital covenant. Keep your wife's back by not talking behind it.

What are our obligations to in-laws?

You should always behave in a Christian manner toward them. Even if they don't share your faith or values, you should forgive them when they offend you, pray for them despite your hard feelings, and never blur the lines between what you owe to your spouse versus what you are willing to give to your in-laws.

Honoring your family and your in-laws is one of God's Ten Commandments. It is stated twice in the Old Testament, because it's that important.

Honor your father and your mother, so that you may live long in the land the Lord your God is giving you.
Exodus 20:12 & Deuteronomy 5:16

You must show them patience, kindness, and respect. You don't have to like them, but God commands you to honor them. Honoring doesn't mean becoming their floor mat or punching bag, but it doesn't mean throwing blows either.

Prior to marriage was your opportunity to get to know the in-laws. If the relationship was strained before marriage, there is no expectation that it would magically improve. That would've been the time to create a plan for managing the intrusion of toxic in-laws.

If you don't get along, and it's hurting your marriage, setting boundaries may not help the relationship, but it may save your marriage.

What are acceptable limits that allow you to still honor them?

1. You are not required to submit yourself to doing things their way.
2. You are not required to allow them to disrespect or control you, your spouse, or your kids.
3. You are not required to obey their advice or requests.

Sometimes the best way to show honor to your in-laws or parents is to say, "No." They may understand you have your own family and priority, or they may be hurt. Either way, your marriage is priority. I live by the apostle Paul's instructions for getting along. Of course, he ends it with, "If it is possible..."

Live in harmony with one another. Do not be proud, but be willing to associate with people of low position. Do not be conceited. Do not repay anyone evil for evil. Be careful to do what is right in the eyes of everyone. If it is possible, as far as it depends on you, live at peace with everyone.
Romans 12:16–18

Fences

Good fences make good neighbors.

Boundaries are there to protect what is valuable to you and your spouse. Both of you must communicate your Position Statement to each family.

A Position Statement is a written guide that lists what you will and will not accept from each family.

Examples:

Interfering in faith and religious services of children (grandparents have been known to get children baptized without parents' consent).

Interfering in child-rearing. If kids stay over with family, they should exercise the same practice as when the kids are at home (diet, movies, use of car seats, etc.).

Giving money to their child in secret to keep from spouse.

Giving ultimatums (It's either your spouse or your blood.).

What if your spouse sides against you? This is a difficult situation. It's hard to break free from parental control, but again there should have been signs before marriage.

If not:

Ensure your spouse knows they are your priority.

Ask if you are their priority.

Communicate your expectations that your spouse side with you.

You and your spouse draft the Position Statement. Hold them to it.

Protect your children from toxic or harmful behavior even if it means your spouse goes to family events alone. (Example: alcoholism, abuse, vulgar language in their home.)

Pray God resolves the situation.

Signs that your in-laws are toxic and the solutions:

- They butt in (limit what they know about your marriage).
- They're mean (honor them, but restrict access).
- They pick sides (avoid allowing them into your marriage conflicts).
- They disrespect your time and space (do not respond to messages and limit time in your home).
- They ignore you (talk one-on-one to them so they must pay attention).

- They treat you like a child (let them know you can handle it and thank them for offering).
- They gossip (let them know you heard they were talking about you).
- They expect too much from you (Once you begin jumping through hoops for them, it will never end. Talk with them.)

Let's wrap this up by remembering this—putting your spouse first causes your marriage to last.

Choosing Friends Biblically

Who are the people in life that immediately darken your door? I'm talking about the kind of people Jesus Christ Himself could've opened the door for them, and they'd gripe because they had to walk around Him. I hate to say it, but you know it to be the truth—cops are some of the most justifiably cynical people on the planet.

While that skepticism is good for keeping us alive on the streets, it's toxic when it becomes part of the fiber of their character. Someone who I considered my best friend for decades was that guy. When I called to share that my son was born, he complained because he had to work late. On the rare occasions I confided in him that something was bothering me, he'd gripe because he didn't get promoted. He's a great guy, but like so many behind the badge, it's a 24/7 pitch-a-fit fest.

It's vital that you carefully select who you're going to invest your life's time with. This goes beyond you, because now your circle must include those who respect your spouse. It's important to surround yourself with positive, affirming, honest people. Culturally, we're the sum of those closest to us.

So if we walk among those who stir strife and darkness, how do you think that affects you? I believe in this:

"Show me your friends, and I'll show you your future."

Walk with the wise and become wise, for a companion of fools suffers harm.
Proverbs 13:20

Don't hesitate to walk away from people who don't share your values. We want to clarify this statement because it's not meant to be like the mean girls on social media who block people because they don't agree with their opinion. No, this is real life, and if someone is intentionally critical of your marriage, then that person has got to go.

Leah and I learned this from our dear friends, Toni and Casey. They regularly assess who they will allow into their inner circle. That means some people get moved out. Maybe those who got moved out of the inner circle remain acquaintances, or co-workers, but our friends are very intentional about relationships. It's been a great lesson for us, and one we set into practice years ago. Don't be anyone's fool. Choose your friends biblically.

One who has unreliable friends soon comes to ruin,
but there is a friend who sticks closer than a brother.
Proverbs 18:24

Friends Who Add Benefit

Who's got your six? This is a question you should regularly ask yourself. It's especially important in cop culture because relationships shift rapidly. Most of your friends are going to be other cops. Eventually, we'd estimate within a few years on the job, the only people LEOs do anything with are other LEOs. But thanks to promotions, assignments, scattered shift work, and attrition, those friendships might wear a badge, but the people behind it change regularly.

You and your spouse should both be asking what friends have your six. It's a great way to practice active transparency and ensure you're plugged into what's going down at cop central. It's not as simple as asking who has your six on the street.

Who has your six when it comes to making good decisions? Or speaks life into your marriage when times get tough, instead of telling you to file for divorce or that there's someone better out there for you? It's important to share with each other who is in your inner circle and who is in your work circle, and whether or not those two circles intersect.

I wanted to take the lead on this section because it's something that affected me so profoundly, and it actually changed my entire life. It applies whether we're married or single, because it's about the nature of cops and men.

Another typical Friday afternoon found me wrapping up paperwork in hopes of heading out of the sheriff's office on time. Although it was over fifteen years ago, I recall very clearly the feeling of despair as I sat at my desk and scrolled through my contact list.

It had been a busy week in the world of commanding a special ops unit, and the last thing I wanted to do was sit at home alone—again. Surely in the list of hundreds of contacts, there had to be a big group of close friends ready to hang out and have the kind of fun they do on the beer commercials.

As I scrolled, I became more and more aware that I was alone. No kidding, in that sea of numbers, there were only four people who were not cops or family. Honestly, I didn't have a clue who most of them were, but what I did know was that they weren't my friends, nor were they hanging out with me on a Friday night. I was alone.

How'd it happen? I had partners at work and buddies in the gym. I also rode with a local bicycle group and trained for triathlons with about four other people. But the guys at work were cops, my workout partners were cops, the people I cycled with almost daily were cops, and every triathlon I competed in, I trained and traveled with cops.

Why?

Because I thought cops were the only people who "got" me. We had a saying—"No apologies needed between cops." I thought that was the gold seal for friendship, when in fact, it was just another avoidance of actual friendship and emotional investment.

That's what I preferred, and although I'd advised younger officers to find an unrelated hobby and circle of friends, I had slowly, and unknowingly, eliminated everyone from my social circle. Except for cops.

That brings me to the circle. Who's in your circle? Without rattling off people you work with, or family, list five people who are really true friends. Not an acquaintance. But a friend in whom you'd confide your most trusted secrets. Someone who you'd allow to see you cry, fail, or be at your weakest.

We wear masks among acquaintances. Although they might lift your couch on moving day, are they the ones you'd trust with making your own death notification to your parents?

There's a social theory referred to as "Who's in your five?" It's based on the ideal that we are the composite of the five people closest in our life. But work partners or casual acquaintances have little to no effect because there's a filter in those relationships that prevents their having influence over your life.

In that isolated season of my life, I wouldn't have been able to name two people, much less five, who were actual friends for the sake of companionship and not a job connection.

During my research, I learned that most men have either one or no close friends at all. As social media continues to separate us from the real world of actual, intimate relationships with real people, the number of adults with no friends has risen from 36 percent to almost 54 percent.

Unless you're fresh out of school and in your twenties, our constricting circle becomes defined by accolades, achievements, academics, and our kids. Promotion and rank add an extra loss of connections because it truly is lonely at the top.

Friendships require vulnerability. Without it, there can never be an intimacy between you. This is where the distinction of friends and acquaintances is most profound. The latter have bonds of loyalty, mutual admiration, and even sacrifice, but beyond occupational obligations, the absence of intimacy is where lines are drawn at the job, the gym, or the gang who heads out for after-work happy hour.

Most of us purposely keep others at a stiff arm's distance. Once we've been on the job a while, it becomes the standard position for immediate family, parents, and siblings, as well as anyone else.

We isolate ourselves, and while we may stand in formation with hundreds of brothers and sisters in blue, we are alone. But friends are just a greeting and call away. Actually, there are lots of cops sitting at home alone right now because of divorce, addiction, depression, and they would give anything for a friend.

Being alone isn't the biblical standard for men. God created us for relationship. With Him, and with each other. Good friends challenge us and call us on the junk in our lives. They care less about our salary and more about our souls.

I know it's tough to reach out to make friends. As we get set in our ways as adults, it becomes even more difficult. But there is value in relationships outside of the job. Isolating ourselves from civilians doesn't make us special, it makes us alone.

Don't beat yourself up because you can't rattle off five close friends, or even one. It's the cultural norm of isolationism. You're not alone; even the churches are filled with friendless men just hoping to make a connection that'll breathe life back into them. It's why men's ministries struggle to sustain growth or a core membership.

Be a man, and start building your brotherhood. The next time someone offers to grab lunch or a coffee, take them up on it. Add to your five and add to the quality of your life.

Iron sharpens iron; so a man sharpens his friend's countenance.
Proverbs 27:17

13

THE ABCS OF MARRIAGE

Accountability

I was first assigned a command position in August of 1992. It was over a large multi-jurisdictional drug task force. I knew nothing, and I mean nothing, about command, federal grant funds, drugs, or much else to do with narcotics work. What I did know about was holding myself and others accountable.

In other words, I was a micromanager. I'm not sure if there's a deeper level beyond micro, but if there is, then that was me. I oversaw everything done out of fear of making a mistake. But as I gained experience, mentoring, and confidence, accountability looked less like a process for punishment and more like a system of reassurance.

As a LEO couple, it's vital that you both accept an environment of accountability. We're going to talk about the positive angle to it and not the "gotcha" effect. Too much of that and it devolves into judgment of your beloved's behavior.

What is accountability? A few men I know through the ministry used to describe it as ratting yourself out to God. I used to laugh and tell them that would be confession, but they were close. Although I knew the term ratting out was more of a joke amongst them, the intention of making known what was done, was absolutely on point.

So then each of us will give an account of himself to God.
Romans 14:12

Accountability is an honest reckoning of self-judgment. Your wife should also be there to help monitor with an objective perspective, and gentle, encouraging words. The negative connotation comes from disciplinary uses. Back in grade school, on the job, civil and criminal codes, and in church, all we've ever known is the reactive nature of being held accountable.

No wonder no one wants to hold themselves accountable. When applied in a negative "gotcha" after the fact, it loses its appeal and application for the sake of what we're working to accomplish.

Let's look at accountability another way.

What if we instead looked at accountability in a positive light? If instead of it being a tool to retro-discover failures, we front-load success by clearly identifying the expectations ahead of time, and then apply accountability measures as a means to progressively monitor and guide the entirety of the marriage journey.

I am not, and never will be a good runner. Especially not a fast runner. Even while training for triathlons and half marathons, my running philosophy was start slow, end slower. But in run training, the timed splits are vital. They are a front-end goal loaded for potential success.

Let's say you are running the mile on a standard high school track. That will be four laps until you collapse into a heap, sucking air in gratitude that it's done. But if you want to set a new record, then you know that there is a goal pace for running each of the four laps.

Running slow around lap two doesn't mean failure, it just means you have two more laps to pick up the pace so that by the checkered flag, you'll have brought yourself back into alignment with victory. Do they actually wave a checkered flag in running?

I'm not sure because I've never come close to finishing first, but I hope you get the idea. Accountability is important, and scripturally necessary for keeping our marriage on the path toward obtaining intimacy between each other.

We also achieve our goals more often when we work with someone to help us remain accountable. Not a taskmaster, or judge, or disciplinarian, but in the biblical description of how each spouse is to submit to the other. This is why the "leave and cleave" principle of Genesis 2:24–25 is so important to a marriage. Both are created to complement and support the other as one (*Galatians 6:1–5*).

I know you might prefer holding yourself accountable as opposed to opening up to your wife. It's embarrassing to ask for help with a personal problem. It can be downright mortifying to share the details. But God encourages us to not only hold each other accountable, but to also confess our sins to one another for healing. If you can't trust your wife with every single detail of your life, then you're not receiving the blessing of the two-as-one relationship.

Therefore, confess your sins to one another and pray for one another, that you may be healed. The prayer of a righteous person has great power as it is working.
James 5:16

We need each other. One-on-one, in prayer groups, small groups, online ministry, or the many other opportunities to draw closer to each other. Looking at accountability as a path to marital success speaks to the language you both understand. Coming wide open to your wife increases her security and leads to greater intimacy. A husband who knows his wife comes to him with her deepest needs feels respected as the spiritual head of their home.

Boundaries

One of the first things Leah helped me understand in the context of a sound biblical marriage was boundaries. I was like so many of us in public service. My work, reputation, and acceptance among peers was so important, that I couldn't accept the reality of being held within boundaries.

Boundary setting for first responders can be seen as an insult and restriction to the alpha personalities that send us running toward danger while everyone else flees for safety. We are conquerors after all. Like a yard dog with an electronic fence, we don't like being boxed in. Of course, this is also what gets us into most of our troubles.

My wife had a great way of explaining that you create boundaries to protect what you love, while keeping the threats on the outside. She is correct. Boundaries are meant for our protection. Cells are created for our confinement.

There was only one boundary at the very beginning of creation. Adam and Eve were free to roam the entirety of paradise. Talk about a sweet deal. They were placed in charge of everything God had personally created.

> *And God blessed them, and God said unto them, "Be fruitful, and multiply, and replenish the earth, and subdue it: and have dominion over the fish of the sea, and over the fowl of the air, and over every living thing that moveth upon the earth."*
> *Genesis 1:28*

Except for the one and only boundary, Adam and Eve had nothing to worry about. God made it easy, and told Adam to eat from any tree in the garden except the tree of the knowledge of good and evil. With that one boundary set for everyone's own good, God left them to enjoy the literal fruits of His labor. Well, you know how that worked out, right?

The boundaries you both need to secure your marriage will be different based on your own situation. But those protections must be discussed and very clearly identified. There can be no security in misunderstood boundaries. If there has been a history of infidelity or the potential, then those boundaries might include restricting/blocking access to the third party through social media or the workplace. An issue with overspending might include boundaries such as budgeting, and both spouses approving any expenditure over a certain dollar amount. They will be as varied as your personalities are, so take time to explore and set meaningful boundaries to protect, not punish.

Will it be a piece of cake knowing there are limits to selfish desires? No, because satan wants you to cross that line. He can't shove you across it, but he will try to get inside your head to consume your thoughts with nothing else but what's been set outside of your boundary. This is why we want you to understand that there is security and joy within your own boundaries, and also that satan is the father of lies.

We're no different from Adam. We want what we can't have. But there are reasons why we can't have certain "fruits," and of course, there are consequences when we take that bite out of those things that are forbidden.

Following up on the example of Adam and Eve, not only did they violate the boundary and lose their intimate connection with God, but there was another boundary established that they were forbidden to cross. It was the entrance back into the garden of Eden, and this time God ensured it remained beyond their reach with the help of an angel and flaming sword. Yes, some decisions come with greater consequences than others.

How fired up do you think satan was once he saw Adam and Eve on the outside of paradise and God's will? Yep, the same amount of happiness he feels when we stick a tip-toe across the boundaries of our marriage covenant. What are you doing that brings a smirk to satan's face?

When we look at the big picture, I'm not sure why we are so averse to the idea of boundaries. They are everywhere from speed limits on the highway to the number of calories on a diet. Boundaries shouldn't be seen as limits to our fun, but standard bearers for achieving success, or simply having a good, safe time.

Where are you in need of boundaries?

Without an objective perspective, you may not see the people closest to you that serve as triggers for breaking boundaries, locations that remind you of "the good old days," or activities that are just waiting to reel you back to your past. We know you might shy away from this topic because it can get uncomfortable to talk about our weaknesses, but unless we do, those weaknesses will soon cause you to crumble. The only hard talks are those we don't have.

Here's to protecting the good stuff.

Consequences

We always tell our kids, "Decisions and Consequences."

As they grew older, they'd laugh and say, "We know, decisions and consequences." Those two words brought almost as much joy as my three favorite words, "I love you."

Decisions and consequences go together, and if there was any other measure by which to use when deciding between one thing or the other, it's invaluable. For me, personally, it was also confirmation that what I probably repeated a thousand times had actually stuck in their heads.

We've purposefully covered what I like to call the Spiritual ABCs over this section. Accountability and Boundaries were explained and encouraged for use in a positive way for promoting marital success by ensuring each other in the languages of security and respect that we speak.

We're going to flip the concept of consequences upside down. Consequences without teeth really offer little support toward the goal of maintaining accountability within boundaries.

Also, the truth is, consequences are usually out of your control. Criminal actions result in consequences handed out by a judge, work violations are handled by a supervisor, and personal indiscretions are addressed by your spouse or other members.

We can't in good conscience water down the importance of consequences. We face them every day. From waking up late and missing work, to failing to do as your spouse asks and block the person who keeps sending suggestive texts. The only upside is that we really hate receiving discipline, so we try harder to remain on the rails to avoid the punishment of consequences.

If your relationship has reached the point where the consequences no longer matter, it's time for intensive focus because you're dealing with issues that began much earlier than your marriage. Consequences have no influence when pain is so intense, and the need to numb it is so strong that you almost find yourself wanting to get busted in hopes it goes away. We get to a level where we've been hurting for so long that no consequence short of death could make us feel any worse about ourselves.

That's a very dangerous place to fall into. How do we know that there are such serious past pain issues that may be manifesting themselves into problems that are only now hurting your marriage? It's usually when accountability and boundaries are established that these darker issues come to the surface. Please don't allow that to stop you from doing these things. That would be like avoiding the doctor because you got your arm chopped off. Avoiding is not healing.

The problem we face is that we've fought to hide or survive those problems. We've probably hidden them from our wife, so there's been a resilience developed over the years. Our weakness has been calloused for so long that besides being numb, we also become very hardened. The most hurtful thing becomes the reality that we're trapped in that lifestyle, and no matter how bad we want to do better, to feel better, to be better—we can't.

After the defeat of our spirit and the surrender to living a life controlled by our past pain and current efforts to avoid it, how do we use consequences to our benefit? There are certain influencers that motivate us in everything we do.

There are two ways to best use the concept of consequences, since the reality of it has little bearing in our life, or even death. Consider what our actions do to others. Start with a series of concentric circles. Maybe the outside circle includes your work acquaintances. The next ring holds your friends, while the one inside of that includes extended family. Next would maybe be your kids, and the one after that is your spouse. Of course, the smallest and most affected circle is you.

While you can cross out the innermost circle representing yourself because consequences don't move you to change, how about looking at all of the other people in your life who get hurt because you can't pull it together. We'd suggest you actually draw out this visual. It's stunning when you see that there's more than just you invested in your being able to accept and allow accountability and boundaries to handle deeper issues that consequences can't touch.

The other option for helping the concept of consequences to maintain a sense of value in your life is to understand that the entirety of your life is the consequence of other people failing you. This may be the only way for you to comprehend the bigness of just how important consequences are. We're not trying to lay a guilt trip on you, but we won't give up on helping you to pierce your heart for the reality of cause and effect.

Because your marriage troubles may represent the consequences of someone failing or harming you in the past, your relationship of dysfunction has become your normal. If you bring anything away from this message, please let it be this—you are not responsible for what hurt you in the past, but you are responsible for how you respond to it today. Your marriage depends on you taking steps to right whatever wrongs are causing your marriage harm.

We know this section about consequences got a little dark, but the reality of this is that all of us come into marriage with baggage. While some looks like a small tote bag, others carry shipping containers of it. Unless you both remain transparent about your past and are willing to use scriptural accountability as a positive support mechanism within which protective boundaries are established, then consequences may lead to personal and relational darkness.

Stay in the light of Christ.

Avoiding is Not Winning

Years ago, Leah and I were in a tough spot. I mean we were getting hammered from every angle, including each other. She was worrying about whether I was going to walk out of the door, and I was worrying why it was that she didn't want me to leave. Truth was, neither of us were ever going to give up on each other.

We were in a season of utter darkness. We'd experienced death, loss of family, separation from friends, financial crisis, health threats, continuing custody battles, and our marriage that was built on empty words and lies was imploding before our eyes.

It's funny, but as soon as I typed the phrase "utter darkness" I felt God move to correct that. There was a light that continued to shine throughout that year. Sometimes it was a pinprick, while other times it was blisteringly bright. But the one constant was there was always a light.

One morning while we prayed together, crying out in despair at the latest volley of attacks, the Holy Spirit simply said, "Avoiding is not winning." Now, I'm a sports guy, and I understand that winning takes effort, but I never thought about it as something to avoid or not avoid. What was God saying to us?

I have a habit of checking my emails as soon as I get out of bed. After months of mounting pressure and personal attacks, I finally stopped looking at the hundreds of emails that had piled up in my account. I'd been avoiding them out of fear because of the constant stream of bad news.

I was avoiding the realities of our actions, and of course, the consequences that followed. But hiding in a dark corner solves nothing, and God knew it was time to come back into the light.

That day changed everything. Being accountable in all things is as important as being accountable to each other. Sure, it's hard to worry about anything else while your life and marriage are falling apart, but the reality is, life goes on. We're in a tough profession that doesn't allow us the option of avoiding dangerous scenarios. Your marriage should get the same level of focused attention when it comes to managing risks, prioritizing actions, and giving your most important partner everything you've got.

It will take a while to dig your relationship out from tough times. How long did it take you to sink into them? Consistency is the key. Refusing to avoid the issues that are causing the problems is what God placed on my heart that morning, and it's so important that we share it with you. If it's addiction, don't avoid it. If it's adultery, don't avoid it.

If its financial debt, don't avoid it. If it's unbelief in God, don't avoid it.

There is no perfect marriage, but the best ones come from two people who refuse to avoid, surrender, or fail. You two be those people!

14

FORGIVENESS

Ed sat in my police cruiser as tears flooded his cheeks. He wafted between outrage and desperate for answer, and I promised him we'd drive around until he was ready to return to the office. But truth be told, he was in no condition to return to work. He and Julie had been married almost four years, and he was one of those guys who beamed with pride over being a husband and dad.

The guy Julie had been having an affair with since before she and Ed were married reached out to Ed because he and Julie had a lover's spat. To say the least, Ed was justified in his devastation. That day in my cruiser wasn't the time to talk about forgiving his wife, but instead, it was the time to listen to a wounded friend.

In the days to come we talked about forgiveness and how it was important for allowing him to move forward. Forgiving her didn't mean he approved of what she had done, and it wasn't for letting her off the hook. Freedom through forgiving others is for you. It sets the captive free from what was done to harm you.

Sure, he had the legal and biblical authority to divorce her, but his heart wasn't ready to break from his commitment to her. Instead, he chose to forgive her. I was amazed over time as I watched him free himself from the pain and shame created by his wife's decisions to cheat, and for him to turn that freedom back into love and blessings for his wife.

They spent the next year in counseling, but my bet is they'll spend the rest of their lives in marriage. Had Ed not truly forgiven his wife for what she had done to hurt him, he would've never had the freedom of choice to keep the family together through spiritual and marital reconciliation. Oh, and as of writing this book, they've had their second daughter.

The simple answer to why we forgive is because God said so. But if you're like me, saying that does about as much good as being told to eat my veggies. We'd like to take this opportunity to walk you through the process of how priceless forgiving actually is. And just in case you're wondering what God has to say about forgiving others, let this sink in a bit:

For if you forgive others their trespasses, your heavenly Father will also forgive you, but if you do not forgive others their trespasses, neither will your Father forgive your trespasses.
Matthew 6:14–15

So how does this relate to cops? Well, in this case, forgiving applies to us just the same as it applies to everyone else. It's nonnegotiable, and we can't outwork it or fix it. This is a gift from God, and we'll not, and I repeat, we will not ever know freedom until we forgive those who have sinned against us.

Forgiving is about freedom. Your freedom, not the offender's freedom. Forgiveness gives you the power to break the chains that bound you into torment, anger, hatred, or the hell of victimization. God gives you the ability to regain the power through surrendering to His command of forgiving. Some see it as weakness, and that's an unfortunate mistake. Forgiving is about power and control you can exercise over your life.

No matter how hopeless or lost you may feel, forgiving those who hurt you gives you strength through Christ. God is very clear that He will forgive you and bless you once you've released yourself from the sin committed against you by another person. You don't even have to say it to the offender. You must, however, speak the words aloud. Go into your private prayer place, or take a drive around the block in your cruiser, but God wants to hear your words of forgiveness.

Let's narrow this down to the most important person on this earth —your wife. They often suffer the most and rarely get the recognition for it. They become a consenting or tolerating police widow while you're out saving the world or just hanging out after shift.

If you've hurt your spouse through neglect, abuse, or adultery, then it's you who must receive forgiveness. If she was the offender, then you must forgive her. We know it's hard because emotions are in the mix. Pride, ego, control, and often a taste for revenge are all the devil's handiwork. And, because we are human, we can expect to get hurt or hurt each other's feelings every now and then. That's why forgiving is an active process that restores your love connection, security, and intimacy. Give it a shot.

Fighting to Forgive

We don't take the act of forgiving lightly. It might be the most difficult thing we do. I mean, won't ignoring the person have the same effect? We all know the answer to that. No.

I have a good friend that Leah and I came to meet through an article I'd written for *Law Enforcement Today*. The article was about healing from past pain and forgiveness. It focused on forgiving the other cops who tend to stab us merciless in the back. If you've been on the job for at least a week, you know what I'm talking about.

If you don't know what I'm talking about, ask your wife. They're very intuitive and their objective distance from outside of the culture allows them to see the truth behind veiled intentions. It's a jungle out there, but it's often more dangerous in the squad room.

Anyway, my friend from Texas had responded to a call for service one night. Upon arrival, he was blasted point blank in the face with a shotgun. He shares that the shooting didn't hurt him as much as the reception from other officers in his own agency did. He wanted to meet me not because of his story of having forgiven his shooter (which he did), but about his struggle in forgiving his brothers in blue. His story is one of incredible service, sacrifice and survival.

The job can be the best of environments, and just as quick, it can turn into a cesspool of deception and undermining your every decision. It's no wonder attrition rates remain so high for policing. The stress of carrying around all of that unforgiveness is unbearable and a huge risk to your life, and marriage. Not convinced? Ask your wife.

Try actively forgiving those who hurt you in the squad room, and you will see a major difference in the way you develop a spiritual immunity to their jabs and attacks. The main reason cops fight to fit in is to avoid being picked on or hazed.

Trust us, it's not just you feeling the dump truck of inter-office anxiety. Your spouse and family suffer from it too. How? Because you come home and dump on them. Free yourself and spare those you love. We want to break this next part up into two sections because the effect of law enforcement is so powerful that there is a need to practice professional and personal forgiveness. The intersections have influence on both, and the potential to destroy either.

Professional Forgiveness

I'm astounded by the depth of hurt within our blue fraternity. Hurt people, hurt people. Pain and unforgiveness travel across multilane expressways in the ranks of policing. Unfortunately, there are no caution signs or stoplights as we hate and hurt out of control until we crash.

It's an alpha environment where the wolves devour sheep, even if they wear the same uniform. The uniqueness of cop culture is that we bond together to fight the external enemy, but when none exist, we cannibalize each other. It's constant drama in the squad room. Whether it's about preferential assignments, who got the primo off-duty details, grant OT, or who's sleeping with who, it gets messy amongst the brotherhood.

This is where the jabs go just below skin deep, so anger and resentment build up, but not bubble over. Instinctively, we suck it up without confronting each other because we're brothers of the badge, and that's what we're supposed to do, right? All that does is create a wounded spirit. We then become what?

Hurt people.

And then we do what?

Hurt people.

I understand that you've got to pick your battles with co-workers, so what are your options for escaping from the resentment of inner-office hurt? Forgiveness is the answer. It's an old saying, and it is true —he who angers you, controls you. Don't allow anger to build. You'll make yourself miserable at work, which will contribute to you not being able to fulfill your duty obligations, experience chronic illness and injuries, experience emotional suppression that may lead to clinical depression, and yes, believe it or not, even suicide.

Why do you think domestic violence committed by cops on their family is so prevalent? Would you ever imagine someone entering the basic academy years ago with the career goal of beating his wife and then killing both her and himself? Google it and you'll see more than you might ever want to know. It's not random. It's a by-product of pent-up frustration, rage, and unforgiveness. The emotional balloon will only stretch so far before it blows.

The best investment you can make right now is to start a practice of speaking power and God's authority over you and your wife. This purposeful act of marital reinforcement will help defend you both by regaining control of a life from those who have snared grappling hooks in your family's spirit.

This goes for your wife too. It's easy to take on secondary trauma. I used to tell Leah details of everything from murders to adversarial city council meetings. I didn't realize the damage it was causing her. I was actively engaged in the conflict, so at the very least, I was able to process the details through action. Leah was trapped with only the information and no way to process it. You may have found yourself in that same situation of your venting, causing her harm long after you've hopped to the next radio call for service.

It's important for them to forgive even the wounds caused by secondary trauma.

By forgiving, you are not allowing the guilty party off the hook like some district attorney desperate for reelection, and you sure don't want to play with the contrived mysticism of karma for getting even. We have no authority to police on behalf of God. He's fully capable of handling spiritual violators on His own. Matter of fact, I'd much prefer God handle it. In other words, let it go and get out of God's way.

Avenge not yourselves, beloved, but give place unto the wrath of God: for it is written, Vengeance belongeth unto me; I will recompense, saith the Lord.
Romans 12:19

Personal Forgiving

Did you ever make the mistake of wearing the same clothes home after OC spray or gas training? It didn't take long until everyone realized what a huge mistake that was. All because you aren't sneezing and coughing with burning eyes doesn't mean your spirit isn't being attacked. The posture of unforgiveness and grudge-holding erupts far beyond the tour of duty or the gas house. It invades our personal relationships and causes stress for everyone involved.

Too often LEO marriages endure injuries that each other aren't even aware of. So much time is spent apart, that absence becomes the offense. Cops don't stop to consider that the void in their marriage is creating a toxic environment for those abandoned at home. Because of this, we must work to release ourselves from the emotional injuries by forgiving others. It's easier said than done, but it's important to stop fighting against forgiving and start rewarding yourself with freedom (*Mark 11:25*).

It might be a special dinner gone cold, or the errand you forgot to run, but no matter what the act was, you're responding with an emotional prompting curated by seething agitation, disappointment, and unmet expectations. This is where satan begins to noodle his way into your life, and temptation slithers in to start planting seeds of doubt, suspicion, or irrational jealousy.

Without forgiving your wife for the hurts she has caused you and vice versa, those gaps can destroy your relationship. Of course, we aren't suggesting you become a doormat that forgives without confronting the offenses, but unless you first clear your heart of the emotions all tied up inside, the mature conversation meant to clear the air will usually erupt into more upheaval.

Within an atmosphere of forgiveness, comes reconciliation between two. Spirit-led conversations take on an entirely different tone when approached with a slate where unforgiveness no longer exists.

God's instruction to not only forgive, but to bless others goes for your blessings as well. Give it a try, and we know you'll both experience success with communicating instead of steaming over tension-filled silence. Why? Because your spiritual centers are now talking a language of love instead of allowing unsteady emotional accusations to control your marriage.

When you both stop fighting and begin gracing each other with forgiveness, you will be blessed by the love God created marriage to enjoy. Does your marriage reflect this standard for love? If it does, then God bless you. If not, this is why we're working through this book together.

Love is patient, love is kind. It does not envy, it does not boast, it is not proud. It does not dishonor others, it is not self-seeking, it is not easily angered, it keeps no record of wrongs. Love does not delight in evil but rejoices with the truth.
1 Corinthians 13:4–6

15

AFFAIR RECOVERY

"Never, ever, confess."

That was advice given to me within my first week as a special agent assigned to a large multi-jurisdictional drug task force. I thought how big of a mistake it was to have opted for this mission out of patrol instead of the detective sergeant's position that was offered.

The commander was a long-time drug agent with a checkered, mysterious past. He wasn't all that bad, but he was far away from decent. But in the early years, I was still very optimistic and naïve. There was a need for warriors in a raging drug epidemic, and I wanted to make a difference in the world. Though his words condemning confession had me confused.

It didn't take long until I saw the web of deceit woven throughout the drug task force. My commander was a master spider, and because of his inability to compromise or even show compassion, the team suffered greatly. Young, talented cops willing to lay it on the line for the sake of making lives better for others were forced out, fired, transferred, or quit.

When confronted by internal investigations about his mishandlings of everything from evidence to integrity, that old serpent stuck to his guns and he never, ever, confessed. Thankfully, he was gone less than a week later.

When we lock ourselves into a posture of refusing to forgive, we are forced to cling to whatever is left. Even if that's nothing but lies. Forgiveness allows us a path to freedom from the pain of sin's separation from God's grace. Let's talk about what that freedom looks like and means to your marriage.

Freedom in marriage is sometimes thought to look like a prisoner digging his way beneath the jail's big open yard, past the towers, and below the concertina wire-topped fences. He rustles only enough earth to pop up from the tunnel like a mole. A quick but quiet peek back at his captors before scurrying away into the darkness with old greyhounds howling in the distance.

That's not freedom. That's running from the responsibility for your wrongs. Of course, we all know it's just a matter of time until that old posse recaptures him. But this isn't what freedom through forgiveness is, nor is it the way for us to duck and dive each other when one's been wronged.

Forgiveness in freedom for us came the day Leah asked me one question.

"Are you having an affair?"

"Yes," I answered.

Is the act of truly forgiving someone easy? Of course not, but neither is living captive to unconfessed and unforgiven sin. Leah was finally set free from the darkness of living with the fears and suspicions of infidelity. I was set free from the sexual sin that had me trapped by the same advice that crooked commander once told me—never, ever, confess.

That guy was wrong.

I wanted out of those chains, but I didn't know how to get out. Confession was the key to my freedom, but like most of us trapped behind a wall of secrets, I wasn't sure of what was on the other side. I'd grown to accept that my life would be defined within the walls of captivity to sexual sin.

Leah, on the other hand, knew that freedom was available through

God's grace. She also knew that confession, forgiveness, and repentant restoration were the key to my dungeon's door. Trust me, you will never know true mercy until you hear the sincere spoken words of your loving spouse say, "I forgive you."

Those three words showed me that law enforcement's code of silence only applies to information and informants, but not to your wife and family. Secrets are intimacy killers, and do not belong between husbands and wives.

Honestly, I didn't know how she could've forgiven me, but that is where God's grace covered her with the spiritual ability to forgive. It's not a natural decision, but a supernatural commitment to release herself of the hurt I created by the harm I caused.

Our freedom began with my repentant heart and her forgiving me. And it allowed us to move forward into an atmosphere of repair over the next year of intense Christian counseling. Had she not forgiven me, those sessions would've just been wasted hours sitting on opposite ends of a couch while she wilted with bitterness and I agonized in guilt.

By God's grace, forgiveness had set her free from those toxic feelings and allowed her to gain trust in her confidence of my commitment to our marriage.

That was a tough year. Although I agreed to attend counseling, I went because I wanted to save our relationship, but I didn't really plan on participating all that much.

Guess what? I found myself sharing things I'd never shared with anyone but Leah before. I cried, and I healed. Forgiving yourself is an important step toward freedom from sin. You're no good to anyone else unless you're first good to you. I knew I'd packed a lot of baggage over the years on the job, but I had no clue how destructive it was or would continue to be.

What that experience also showed both of us, and it applies to you as well, is that there must be a trust established between both spouses. That trust is like a level landing pad where, no matter what the topic or the offense, it's entered into with a confidence that no grudges are held or past hurts resurfaced.

The freedom through forgiveness is a radical challenge for us men. We're not naturally inclined to tell on ourselves, nor or we quick to apologize. Between an unrealistic expectation to get it right, and our wife's wishful expectation that we should always get it right, we find ourselves in an unenviable demigod position.

That shaky pedestal won't last, and because men are hesitant to confess when forgiveness is needed, we remain perched on a broken branch of selfish refusals and dangerous denial. A safe place to seek forgiveness removes the hesitation of being seen as weak.

When apologies come easy because both of you trust that repair and restoration are the goal, the soft words short-circuit potential implosions. This common place of communication is also a result of a shared mutual respect for each other.

Again, for men, many of us have that unintended chauvinistic gene buried somewhere in our old-school DNA. My dad dominated my mom and all of his kids. He discounted her and made decisions for the family without her opinion. That embedded a thread of behavior that surfaced in our own relationship. For years I thought it was my take-charge personality, when in fact, it was devaluing Leah as my equal in marriage. It didn't mean I was bad, it just meant I had to do better. We can break that bond to a disrespectful past, and enjoy the mutuality of relationship with our wives.

Freedom through forgiveness also takes the form of transparency. My cell phone held confidential emails and text messages with information about ongoing cases. I maintained the security protocols without fail. But once I retired, there was nothing law-enforcement sensitive on my wiped-clean device. Yet there were still secrets being guarded behind that locked screen.

My wife's forgiveness and restoration graced me with a freedom from secrecy that I'd never known. It was liberating. Sure, it was tense leading up to the moments of confession and repentant reconciliation, but I knew there was nothing worth protecting or fighting for inside that cell phone.

I'll always cherish the day it really stuck for me. My fourteen-year-old daughter and I were going to get ice cream, and she wanted to share a new music artist with me. I handed her my phone, and since I'd already given her the passcode, she zipped it open and began to scroll through it until she found the song and a few funny family pics.

Liberation is having the freedom through transparency to hand your cell phone over to your wife or curious teenage daughter with zero fear of exposure, or an untimely text. It also allows for great music to play while heading to get ice cream.

Praying Together

I wanted to do it but I just couldn't. Leah and I were praying separately and we'd both enjoyed a strong connection to God through prayer. But when it came time to connect in prayer as a couple, I couldn't do it.

The first few times I just thought it would take a little getting used to. After a month, I knew there was a problem. As the spiritual head of our home, it was my responsibility and honor to lead my wife in communication with God. I couldn't, but why not?

Praying together as a couple would seem like the most natural act between two people who love each other. Taking it a step further, how about two believers who love each other and engage in an active prayer life?

While it would also appear praying together would be just as much a part of the loving relationship as saying, "I love you," it often becomes a sticking point in relationships.

Why is it so difficult?

Time

Time, or the absence of it, is the most often-cited reason for not praying together as a couple. While there may be legitimate occasions where extreme schedules prohibit praying together, those moments are rare.

Praying together doesn't require all day marathon prayer sessions.

A genuine five-minute investment of spirit-filled time in God's presence is worth more than any business meeting or busy schedule.

- Where to find the time:
- Wake up ten minutes earlier.
- FaceTime each other over lunch.
- While waiting for your kids at practice.
- Before bedtime.
- After sex (Seriously. God created sex, and thanks to the chemical release of oxytocin in men, a feeling of intense closeness will make praying more open and sincere.)

Uncertainty

Men usually have a more difficult time initiating couple's prayer. The biblical expectation places man as the head of household. This also means the spiritual leader as well. Most men simply don't know how to get started. If it were a sport or fixing the car, they'd roll up their sleeves and get it done. When it comes to leading his wife in prayer, the proverbial brakes get slammed.

There's an intimidation factor with intimately praying with your wife. What if your prayers are not significant or spoken eloquently enough? How about if you don't say the right things, or you stumble over your words? Is your wife going to lose respect for you?

This is not a case of silence is golden. It's a time for men to ask God for guidance and the words to speak. Praying should make us feel vulnerable. It's God we're talking to after all.

Where men can find the motivation:

- Don't try being courageous.
- Accept that you aren't in charge.
- Expect a blessing for your obedience.
- Know you aren't being judged by your spouse.

Above the Radar

Once a couple goes all out in God's service, it's not uncommon for satan to begin mingling in their affairs. Praying couples mean they're drawing ever closer to Christ. That closeness begins to squeeze out space for temptation and marital strife. That means the relationship is happier and more fulfilling, i.e....bulletproof!

But Christians have admitted to living below the spiritual radar in hopes of avoiding satan's attentions. An uncertain spouse with unconfessed sin may fear unintentional discovery by their spouse or may feel their Achilles heel could become a focal point that brings destruction to the marriage if old habits resurface.

I want to encourage you. This isn't a case of letting sleeping dogs lie. Get in the fight. Armor up with the word of God and allow Him to defeat all of your enemies who stand against your LEO marriage. God will bless your marriage for your faithfulness.

How to Start Praying Together

- Keep your prayers casual.
- Schedule a set time each day.
- Keep your prayers short but to the point.
- Don't worry about memorizing scripture.
- Open your mouth and your heart will follow.
- Ask your wife if there are prayer requests.
- Be sensitive to the Holy Spirit's presence.

God does not expect you to sound like Billy Graham, but He, and your wife, need to hear what is deepest in your heart. Once you start, you'll be so amazed at how quickly the Holy Spirit arrives to guide both of you the rest of the way home.

16

VISIONS OF THE PROMISED LAND

A Marriage Vision

Fail to plan, plan to fail.

How many times have we heard this and thought we'd just work it out along the way? I've held briefing after briefing after briefing, from a highway sobriety checkpoint, to a hostage rescue mission, and planning was always the key.

But even before any of my law enforcement missions were ever executed, a vision had been established for the agency that created an environment for success, no matter what came our way. When it came time to get our hands dirty, all we needed was a plan that worked within the vision.

You are both going to have to roll up your sleeves and get your hands dirty. No marriage is perfect, and the best of them involve two people who refuse to give up on themselves, each other, or their marriage. But just like the best of agencies, there has to be a foundational plan. This structure will benefit your marriage when those tough times come. And trust us, they will come.

There's nothing like a good slogan to rally a team or build your business around. This is also true for marriages. Of course, in this case, the slogan is your marriage's vision statement. It doesn't have to be long or complicated, but it does have to dive into the heart of the matter. This is a pretty good one.

> *But as for me and my household, we will serve the Lord.*
> *Joshua 24:15*

Because you're in a LEO marriage, your time is already demanded by the department, others on your shift or in your squad, the chief, the community, and everyone else who thinks that because of your badge they own a piece of you. This should be enough reason to want to claim ownership of your relationship and create a meaningful vision statement.

Most of us get married and assume once the wedding bash ends, that's also the end of the process. The wedding was just the starting pistol. You have a lifelong race to run with the best partner you'll ever have. But to run that race with success you must lay out a path.

Too many couples bump throughout each day and figure they'll work it out somehow, someday. Meanwhile, each is growing dissatisfied in their own lives and the relationship. Why? Because no one has identified why it is that you are married and what it is that you both want the marriage to look like. Marriages need a common goal. Why are you married? What's your purpose for being married? Can you answer those questions?

If we gave a bunch of people generic uniforms, a nondescript building, and unmarked vehicles with neutral-colored lights, how are you to know whether you're cops, firefighters, EMS or civil patrol? Jeez, you might even be confused for a taxi driver or a mall security guard.

The point is, without purposeful intentionality, you're both only existing as roommates. You have the God-given authority to define who you want to be and what it is that you want to be. Want to be parents? Then write that as your vision statement. Want to travel the world? Then write that as your vision statement. Want to be chief of police? Then write that as your vision statement.

No one can want something more for you than you want for yourself. If you don't make the time to develop one, or if you don't know what you want for your marriage, it's almost impossible to create something meaningful together.

Once you both invest the time to discuss exactly what kind of life, marriage, and family it is that you desire, you'll be able to create a big-picture vision. Once a unified vision is created, you can begin to create goals and objectives toward achieving that vision.

I used to start the daydreaming sessions when I sat in leadership trainings that included pie-in-the-sky sessions of vision statements and other seemingly abstract ideals. But let's look at this in a concrete way.

Let's say your marriage vision is to have a family:

Objective 1: Have kids—define how many.
Goal 1: Have biological kids—if can't, progress to Goal 2.
Goal 2: Adopt kids.
Goal 3: Blend kids from previous relationships—if either has kids.
Objective 2: Stay at home parent.
Goal 1: Secure family income.
Consideration 1: Single family income.
Consideration 2: Supplement main income with home-based business.
Consideration 3: Part-time or second job.
Goal 2: Homeschool kids.
Consideration 1: Time and patience.
Consideration 2: Costs of materials and compliance with policies.
Objective 3: Kids to college.
Goal 1: Open college savings plan.
Goal 2: Choose college prep paths.
Goal 3: Stay informed of changing entrance requirements.
Goal 4: Wave goodbye to kids as they drive off to college.

Okay, this is just a quick example of creating structure within your vision. But the point is, if you want to start a family, there's much more to it than having sex. Can you do it without a vision? Sure you can, and please know that this is a structured support system, and not a rigid plan etched in stone.

I used to tell my SWAT unit that our plan was like a backbone—strong enough to support the mission, but flexible enough to adapt and adjust. Your vision plan should identify what you both want the marriage to look like. The goals and objectives should be used as that guide for every aspect of accomplishing your vision.

Do you want to be a chief of police or sheriff? Trust me, it doesn't just happen. It usually takes years of planning, training, education, and experience, but it all starts with a vision. Yet, unless being the top cop is what you both want, then your chances of obtaining that goal, or any other goal, is compromised. This is why it's critical that you both share your dreams, no matter how big, loud, or unrealistic the other might think they are.

There is no fear, limits, or restrictions in a marriage vision, so go ahead and make your relationship the marriage of your dreams.

Dating Your Spouse

Where has the romance gone?

If you've asked yourself that question before, trust us, you're not alone. There's a psychological light switch that changes our mentality about wooing our spouse the second we say, "I do." Why do we stop trying? Our relationship with each other is the reason we married in the first place.

Marriages have to be nurtured. Have you ever heard the excuse, "We just grew apart," from one of your divorced cop friends? If they'd been dating and putting in quality time with each other to nurture their relationship, chances are, they wouldn't be divorced.

Marriage is to be celebrated, not put on a shelf to gather dust as the years pass. One of the biggest mistakes we made in our marriage early on was not taking the time to celebrate our union. We didn't even take time to honeymoon! We just went back to work and the daily grind.

Neither of us felt like we'd done anything special, and what a disservice that was to God and the holy covenant we made with Him.

Dating is more important during your marriage than it ever was before you got married. Carving out a special time to spend with your spouse tells them you still love them and that you want to be with them. Yes! You do! We promise. If we can do it with five kids at home and our work schedules, you can do it too. We'll give tips for carving out time in the upcoming pages.

It's okay! You don't need money to connect with your spouse. We're going to give you ideas for all different kinds of dates.

The grass is greener where it's watered. What did you talk about before you got married? What made you get that dreamy look in your eyes and stay up until all hours of the night talking? Great communication is key. You might be rusty, but it'll come back like riding a bike.

"I don't have time."

We've been guilty of uttering those words a time or two. I bet you have too. But the truth is, it's not time that's our worst enemy, it's priorities. One of the most important things God did in Genesis was to create Eve, because He didn't want man to be alone.

It is not good that the man should be alone; I will make him a helper fit for him.
Genesis 2:18

Marriage was designed to mirror what our relationship with Christ is supposed to be like. So after our relationship with Christ, marriage is our next priority. Even before our children. The greatest gift you can give your children is parents that have a healthy marriage. This also means your marriage should come before work, bills, friends, school, and Facebook.

There are nights where we'll put the kids to bed, hop in the Jeep, and go get ice cream just so we can spend twenty minutes alone together. If you look for the time, you'll find the time.

Tips for Making Time:

- Make your marriage a priority.
- Get in sync! Coordinate your calendars.
- Schedule at least thirty minutes of alone time (no kids!) where the two of you can check in with each other, and see if there are any issues.
- If your kids are little and you have trouble finding babysitters, schedule one date night per month. Trade babysitting time with other couples in lieu of spending money.
- Make it a goal for date night to become a weekly occurrence. Chances are, when you start to prioritize, you'll be able to find an hour or two for your spouse.

Money and Dating Your Spouse

Is there anything less romantic than a conversation about money? The fact is, money is one of the leading causes of divorce. Date nights to reconnect with your spouse shouldn't be about money, especially if this is a hot button topic for you. Don't break the bank dating your spouse. Adding debt to the problem won't make for an enjoyable date night.

Free Date Night Ideas

An indoor picnic—spread a blanket in front of the fireplace (even in summer!), open a bottle of wine, and have a light meal and great conversation. Steal a few kisses along the way.

Movie night—curl up on the couch and snuggle while watching a movie. Popcorn is optional.

Stargazing—lay a blanket on the ground and look up at the stars. It's a great time to talk about your dreams for the future.

Take a scenic bike ride. Extra points if you pack a picnic to take with you.

Have a pool? Go skinny-dipping!

Video game night. There's nothing like a competitive game of *Mario Kart* to get the blood pumping. It's fun to be a kid again.

Go window-shopping. It's fun to dream big together.

Take a luxury sports car out for a test drive. Have fun!

The library—if you love to read as much as I do, this is an awesome date.

Heat things up in the kitchen. Make a romantic dinner for two together.

During the holiday season, ride around and look at Christmas lights. Bring a thermos of hot chocolate.

Have a backyard campout. Make a fire and cook s'mores. Pitch a tent and share a sleeping bag.

Find a scenic location and watch the sunset together.

More Date Ideas

Painting with a Twist (We love it!).

Dress up in your finest and eat at a fancy restaurant.

Go to a soda shop and share a milkshake with two straws.

Go ice-skating.

Charter a boat for a romantic sunset sail.

Go to a drive-in movie. Sneak kisses when it gets dark.

Play golf, even if you're bad. Sometimes being bad makes it more fun.

Recreate your very first date.

Meet at a coffee shop separately and pretend you're meeting for the very first time.

Go to a wine and cheese tasting.

Make a date at the shooting range and have a target competition.

Go to an arcade and be kids again.

Find a traveling carnival and kiss at the top of the Ferris wheel.

Get a hotel room and order room service. Wake up to watch the sunrise together.

Have a couple's spa day and relax.

Communication and Reconnection

Remember when you hung on to her every word? When you'd talk for hours on the phone, or drift off to sleep just as the sun was starting to rise because of great conversation? That connection is still there, but sometimes it's hard to recognize when you have children, or stresses, like bills and work.

Maybe it's been so long since you've been on a date together that you feel like two strangers with nothing in common. Here's a few icebreakers to get you going:

1. If you could give your younger self one piece of advice, what would it be?
2. What's the most adventurous thing you've ever done?
3. If money was no object, what's one vacation destination you'd like to go to?
4. What's your favorite memory of our wedding day?
5. How can I pray for you?
6. If you could choose any career, what would it be?
7. How often would you like to have sex?
8. Is there anything you've always wanted to do during sex?
9. What's your best memory with one of your parents?
10. Do I have any of the same qualities as your mother/father?
11. What kind of legacy would you like to leave for our children?
12. What's a song that describes our marriage?
13. What's your most embarrassing moment?
14. What's your favorite movie of all time?
15. Do you have a bucket list? What are some things on it?

Let's Wrap It Up

Remember when you'd walk across glass to get a glimpse of your sweetie? What happened? Don't ever forget what it was that drew you together. In fact, do those things often. The truth is, marriage takes time and effort. If you struggle with connecting with your spouse, we've been where you are, and we understand that sometimes things seem hopeless.

Making your marriage a priority is the most important thing you can do after having a relationship with Christ. We want to encourage you that, no matter what season of marriage you're in, you can have a blessed, happy, and whole life with your spouse. Dating your spouse again will reopen with doors of communication, and set you on the path toward success in your marriage.

Here are just a few benefits of being in love:

Physical Changes—Love has physiological effects on your body. Chemical levels, such as dopamine, testosterone, norepinephrine, histocompatibility complex (MHC), and pheromones shift. These are all positive benefits. Dopamine is the brain's pleasure chemical; oxytocin is the bonding/intimacy chemical. Hugging and kissing are important. Testosterone is in both male and females, though higher in males. It ups your sex drive. Norepinephrine increases arousal and alertness, promotes vigilance, enhances formation and retrieval of memory, and focuses attention.

Perspective—Love shifts your self-centered worldview into a shared, or partner-focused, lens. Learning to see the world through another person's heart is a powerful experience. It becomes a more transparent process as trust and love deepens.

Fighting Clean—Single people fight for one thing—preservation for their way of life. Throw a monkey wrench in their machinery and they come out fighting like an angry cat mistakenly bathed by a toilet's flush. Love softens the heart for considering someone else's point of view, and the potential for understanding that the world really doesn't revolve around you. Example: praying together.

Sexier Sex—Intimacy and trust lead to increased sexual pleasure. While being single and ready to mingle might make for a great beer commercial campaign, the reality of lonely nights, untrustworthy partners, or revolving-door relations eventually leads to sexual dissatisfaction. Monogamy, trust, and transparency stimulate intimacy which leads to the type of sex God designed for us—marriage bed super sex.

A Better You—Let's face it, when it's only you that you have to please, becoming self-consumed is almost guaranteed. Without outside stimuli, rare is the occasion to grow or improve. Because it is God's expressed will that two people should become one, it's not only pleasing to Him, but immeasurably pleasing to you.

...AND THAT'S NOT ALL

Less Stress—Married people have less dramatic responses to psychological stress.

Richer—Married people experience a net worth of 77% more wealth per person than single people. Married people also gain significantly more wealth than divorced people.

Safer—Married people take fewer risks, including substance abuse, and live happier, with better health benefits.

Survive—Better cancer survival rate than single or divorced.

Live Longer—Living with a partner lowers the mortality rate for men by 80 percent and for women by 59 percent. Cohabitation before marriage actually reduces the lifespan according to statistics.

Happily Ever After

Leah and I always have the hardest time when it comes to the end of a book. It's the same way when we have to say goodbye to our marriage life group we host at home. We know they'll be back for the next small group meeting, but the bonds built through information, sharing, and prayer connect us all to one another. Of course, it should be difficult to close because we've been through so much with you.

But in the same way we always make sure friends leave our home with food, snacks, or at least a plastic cup full of tea, we want to bless you with the truths of why we began this journey with you and what you can expect to find up ahead as you walk together.

Is there such a thing as happily ever after? Yes. You can be sure of this because it was God Himself who created marriage. God has never created anything to fail. Marriage is the way He relates to us, so it is designed to be lasting. How we support it, partake of it, and honor that relationship is up to us.

It's the same way with our marriage. It was designed by God so that we'd care and support one another; enjoy relationship with our suitable mate; and love, honor, and cherish them as the special gift that they are from God.

We've tried to share so many reassurances as well as warnings about the pitfalls of police marriage. Please don't let it throw you. Being unaware is just as dangerous to your marriage as the dispatch not telling you that there is a felony warrant for the guy you just stopped for speeding. Use this information and learn from experience to not only avoid the mistakes, but to increase the intimacy of your relationship.

It's easy to allow yourself to get caught in the trap of cop culture's promiscuity, divorce, and remarriages. We call it the marriage-go-round. We know you've heard this before, but the only ones who win in divorce are the attorneys. But in reality, satan is the big winner. He hates marriages and will continue to do everything to destroy them.

If you'd take an honest assessment of the problems in your marriage, you'd soon see that sin and satan have had an incredible influence. Otherwise, there'd be no cause for destructive conflict if God was placed at the head of your marriage and family. Yes, there will be disagreements, anger, and problems between you both, but that's natural and expected. We've mentioned Paul's words before about high emotions, and they're worth sharing again.

"Be angry, and do not sin":
do not let the sun go down on your wrath.
Ephesians 4:26

What usually gets in the way of a true happily ever after is the misconception that couples share about having problems. Most think that if they were "meant to be," then they'll never argue, slam a door, or refuse to talk it out during a fight. That's a fantasy. Couples with the greatest advantage for an everlasting relationship are those who have laid the foundations for communicating with each other no matter the situation or severity.

The best way to structure that foundation is to build your relationship upon the "Having Your Six" principles we discussed in Bulletproofing Your Marriage. These simple rules of marriage are based on God's Word, and have been the golden seal, time-tested truths for a happily ever after relationship. Even if you've been blissfully married for years, these principles of Stance, Grip, Sight Picture, Breath Control, Trigger Control, and Follow-Through promise to increase even the deepest of commitments.

Another resource that helps us daily are the marriage mentors we've grown close to. The reason clichés remain in our lexicon is because there is truth to them. Birds of a feather do flock together. In the most positive sense of this example are the opportunities to watch successful marriages happen in the lives of others who are willing to share their experiences.

Over the years we've connected with so many good folks who live the biblical marriage covenant. Does that mean they're perfect? No, not at all, but it does mean they're perfectly willing to open their hearts as trusted models of marriages that work.

On a side benefit that is so important to your LEO marriage, connecting with non-law-enforcement-related marriage mentors exposes you to people who have nothing to do with law enforcement. That helps ground you and also connects you to the big picture that while your marriage is special, it isn't the only one that requires work.

Once you find yourselves isolated from everyone but cops, the red flags have to wave. This may feel like protected waters, but it's a dangerous place for your marriage. Other people help us to maintain that sense of belonging. The lone wolf ethos looks great in the movies, but it does nothing for a marriage.

Law enforcement has been almost the entirety of my adult life. I love the work and I love the people committed to doing the work. And part of loving something is having the ability to see it for what it is—the good and the bad.

Police work is not bad for marriages, but the trappings of outside expectations and organizational behaviors having nothing to do with enforcing the law can destroy your marriage and your life. Stay informed, alert, and aware of those snares. You and your beloved deserve so much more than becoming yet another blue line statistic.

Finally, please know that Leah and I are praying over you. It takes so much courage and sacrifice to put that badge on every day. It also takes a God-blessed wife to hold the line for their marriage and family. God knows the challenges you've both accepted to not only serve the community, but to serve the kingdom. There is blessing in your marriage. Please allow God's anointing oil of eternal blessing to pour over you and your marriage, and know that He has a wonderful plan for each of you and your marriage. It's God's own promise to you!

"For I know the plans I have for you," declares the Lord, "plans to prosper you and not to harm you, plans to give you hope and a future."
Jeremiah 29:11

ACKNOWLEDGMENTS

When we started thinking of everyone who has played a part in what has become this book, we realized what a special community is involved in marriage ministry.

Leah and I are blessed to stand the gap with so many friends who supported us in marriage and now support each other in the battle to strengthen and save LEO marriages.

A special thank you to Darleen Dixon at Wicked Smart Designs and Imogen Howson for all your work in making our vision a reality.

ABOUT THE AUTHORS

Dr. Scott Silverii and his wife, Leah, have blended seven kids, a French bulldog named Bacon and a micro mini Goldendoodle named Biscuit into a wonderfully unique family. Their passion is helping hurting marriages.

They're the founders of Blue Marriage, a first responder marriage ministry that created the Police Marriage Academy. They are both certified as Marriage On The Rock counselors and SYMBIS facilitators.

Scott, a retired chief of police, holds a PhD from the University of New Orleans and is working toward his Doctor of Ministry at The

King's University. Leah is a New York Times and USA Today bestselling author of over 65 titles.

When not spending time with their kids, they enjoy crossing the country on their motorcycle, or hanging out with friends in their hometown of Dallas, Texas.

An experienced speaker, mentor and confidential accountability partner, Scott and Leah are available for workshops, conferences, and church events. Their complete line of resources can be found at - Five Stones Press (www.fivestonespress.org)

OTHER BOOKS BY SCOTT & LEAH

Favored Not Forgotten: Embrace the Season, Thrive in Obscurity, Activate Your Purpose

Unbreakable: From Past Pain To Future Glory

Retrain Your Brain - Using Biblical Meditation To Purify Toxic Thoughts

God Made Man - Discovering Your Purpose and Living an Intentional Life

Captive No More - Freedom From Your Past of Pain, Shame and Guilt

Broken and Blue: A Policeman's Guide To Health, Hope, and Healing

Life After Divorce: Finding Light In Life's Darkest Season

Police Organization and Culture: Navigating Law Enforcement in Today's Hostile Environment

The ABCs of Marriage: Devotional and Coloring Book

Love's Letters (A Collection of Timeless Relationship Advice from Today's Hottest Marriage Experts)

A First Responder Devotional

40 Days to a Better Firefighter Marriage

40 Days to a Better Military Marriage

40 Days to a Better Corrections Officer Marriage

40 Days to a Better 911 Dispatcher Marriage

40 Days to a Better EMT Marriage

40 Days to a Better Police Marriage

More titles from
Five Stones Press

fivestonespress.org

Made in the USA
Coppell, TX
15 July 2023

19142591R00142